KU-216-549

BE MATURE

Warren W. Wiersbe

Scripture Press

Amersham-on-the-Hill, Bucks HP6 6JQ, England

© 1978 by SP Publications, Inc.
First published in the USA 1978 by Victor Books a division
of Scripture Press Publications, Inc., Wheaton, Illinois, USA

First British edition 1988

ISBN 0 946515 56 5

Scripture quotations in this book are from the *Authorized (King James) Version* unless otherwise
noted. Other quotations are from the *New American Standard Bible* (NASB), © the Lockman
Foundation 1960, 1962, 1963, 1968, 1971, 1972, 1973, 1975, 1977; the *Holy Bible: New
International Version* (NIV), © 1973, 1978, 1984, International Bible Society, used by
permission of Zondervan Bible Publishers; *The New Scofield Reference Bible* (SCO), © 1967 by
The Delegates of the Oxford University Press, Inc., New York; *The New Testament in Modern
English* (PH), Revised Edition, © J. B. Phillips, 1958, 1960, 1972, permission of Macmillan
Publishing Co. and Collins Publishers; *The New Testament in the Language of the People* by Charles
B. Williams (WMS), © 1966, Moody Press, Chicago, Ill.

Cover photo: ACE Photo Agency-London

Production and printing in Great Britain for
SCRIPTURE PRESS FOUNDATION (UK) LTD
Raans Road, Amersham-on-the-Hill, Bucks HP6 6JQ by
Nuprint Ltd, Harpenden, Herts AL5 4SE

CONTENTS

*Dedicated with love and appreciation to
some pastor friends who have been a help
and an encouragement to me:*

Mark Bubeck
Jerome DeJong
William Larkin
Erwin Lutzer
Douglas Stimers

PREFACE

Not everybody who grows old, grows up. There is a vast difference between *age* and *maturity*. Ideally, the older we are, the more mature we should be; but too often the ideal does not become the real.

The result is problems—problems in personal lives, in homes, and in churches. As a pastor, I see more problems in these areas caused by immaturity than by anything else. If Christians would just grow up, they would become victors instead of victims.

The Epistle of James was written to help us understand and attain spiritual maturity: " . . . that ye may be perfect and entire, wanting nothing" (James 1:4b). I like the way J. B. Phillips puts it: " . . . and you will find you have become men of mature character, men of integrity with no weak spots."

I trust that these simple expository studies will help you reach that goal.

Warren W. Wiersbe

1

Time to Grow Up

(JAMES 1:1)

Beginning a study of a book of the Bible is something like preparing for a trip: you like to know where you are going and what you can expect to see. When my wife and I were getting ready for our first visit to Great Britain, we spent many hours reading travel books and poring over maps. When we arrived there, we enjoyed the visit much more because we knew what we were looking for and how to find it.

Perhaps the best way to launch a study of the Epistle of James is to answer four important questions.

Who Was James?

"James, a servant of God and of the Lord Jesus Christ. . ." (James 1:1a) is the way he introduced himself. It was a popular name, a form of the great Old Testament name Jacob. There were several men who bore this name in New Testament history.

James, the son of Zebedee and brother of John.
He was one of the most prominent to bear the
name. He was a fisherman called by Christ to follow and become a disciple (Matt. 4:17-22). He and
his brother John were nicknamed by Christ "sons
of thunder" because of their impulsiveness (Mark
3:17, and read Luke 9:51-56). James was the first of
the disciples to give his life for Christ. He was
killed by Herod in A.D. 44 (Acts 12:1-2).

James, the son of Alphaeus. He was another of
the disciples (Matt. 10:3; Acts 1:13), but very little
is known about him. Matthew (Levi) is also identi-
fied as "the son of Alphaeus" (Mark 2:14), and some
students conjecture that the two men might have
been brothers. There is no indication that this
James wrote the letter we are about to study.

James, the father of Judas the disciple. He is an
even more obscure man (Luke 6:16, KJV, where
"brother" ought to be "father"). This Judas was
called "the son of James" to distinguish him from
Judas Iscariot.

James, the brother of our Lord. He seems to be
the most likely candidate for author of this letter.
He does not identify himself in this way; humbly,
he calls himself "a servant of God and of the Lord
Jesus Christ. . . . " That Jesus had brothers and
sisters is stated in Matthew 13:55-56 and Mark 6:3,
and one of His brothers was named James. (By
"brother," of course, I mean half-brother. Joseph
was not our Lord's father since He was conceived
by the Holy Spirit of God.)

James and the other brothers did not believe in
Jesus during His earthly ministry (John 7:1-5 and
Mark 3:31-35). Yet we find our Lord's brethren in
the upper room praying with the disciples (Acts
1:14). What effected the change from unbelief to

faith? First Corinthians 15:7 indicates that Jesus appeared to James after His resurrection! This convinced James that Jesus truly was the Saviour, and he, in turn, shared this knowledge about Jesus to the other brothers.

James became the leader of the church in Jerusalem. Paul called him "a pillar," in Galatians 2:9. It was James who moderated the church conference described in Acts 15. When Peter was delivered from prison, he sent a special message to James (Acts 12:17); and when Paul visited Jerusalem, it was to James that he brought greetings and the special "love offering" from the Gentiles (Acts 21:18-19).

We have no record in the Bible, but tradition tells us that James was martyred in A.D. 62. The story is that the Pharisees in Jerusalem so hated James' testimony for Christ that they had him cast down from the temple and then beaten to death with clubs. The story also relates that James died, as did His Saviour, praying for his murderers, "Father, forgive them, for they know not what they do."

What kind of a man was James? He must have been a deeply spiritual man to gain the leadership of the Jerusalem church in so short a time. His stature is seen in Acts 15, where he was able to permit all the factions to express themselves, and then bring peace by drawing a conclusion based on the Word of God. Paul, in 1 Corinthians 9:5, suggested that he was a married man. Again, tradition tells us that he was a man of prayer, and this explains the emphasis on prayer in his letter. It was said that he prayed so much, his knees were as hard as a camel's!

James was a Jew, reared in the tradition of the

Law of Moses; and his Jewish legalism stands out in his letter. (Note also Acts 21:18ff, where James asked Paul to help him pacify the Christian legalists in the Jerusalem church.) There are over 50 imperatives in the Epistle of James. James did not suggest —he commanded! He quoted the Old Testament only five times, but there are many allusions to Old Testament passages in the letter.

While still an unbeliever, James must have paid attention to what Jesus taught; in his letter there are numerous allusions to our Lord's sayings, particularly the Sermon on the Mount. Compare these passages:

James 1:2—Matthew 5:10-12
James 1:4—Matthew 5:48
James 1:5—Matthew 7:7-12
James 1:22—Matthew 7:21-27
James 4:11-12—Matthew 7:1-5
James 5:1-3—Matthew 6:19-21

Keep in mind that James led the church in Jerusalem during a very difficult time. It was a time of transition, and such times are always upsetting and demanding. There were many Christian Jews in Jerusalem who still held to the Old Testament Law (Acts 21:20). The temple and its services were still in operation, and the full light of the Gospel of God's grace had not yet dawned. We who have read Romans, Galatians, and Hebrews might be prone to judge these early believers; but we must not. They were saved people, but they were still in the shadows of the Law, moving out into the bright light of God's grace. While there may have been differences in degrees of spiritual knowledge and experience, there was no competition between Paul and those who directed the Jerusalem church (Gal. 2:1-10).

To Whom Did James Write?

". . . To the twelve tribes which are scattered abroad, greeting" (James 1:1b). James wrote to Jews living outside the land of Palestine. The term "twelve tribes" can only mean the people of Israel, the Jewish nation (Acts 26:7). The fact that many Jews lived outside their Promised Land is evidence of the spiritual decline of the nation. God had to scatter them (Deut. 4:25ff). When Peter addressed that huge Jewish congregation at Pentecost, he spoke to men from many different nations (Acts 2:9-11).

James sent his letter to *Christian* Jews. At least 19 times he addressed them as "brethren," indicating not only "brothers in the flesh" (fellow Jews), but also "brothers in the Lord." James was very clear on the doctrine of the new birth (James 1:18). There are times when James also addressed wicked men who were not in the fellowship (the rich, for example, in James 5:1-6); but he did so in order to teach and encourage the saved Jews to whom he sent the letter.

The word *scattered* in James 1:1 is an interesting one. It means "in the dispersion." The term *the dispersion* was used to identify the Jews living outside the land of Palestine. But the Greek word carries the idea of "scattering seed." When the Jewish believers were scattered in that first wave of persecution (Acts 8:1 and 4), it was really the sowing of seed in many places; and much of that seed bore fruit (Acts 11:19ff).

Christian Jews scattered throughout the Roman Empire would have needs and problems of their own. Being Jews, they would be rejected by the Gentiles; and being *Christian* Jews, they would be rejected by their own countrymen. This letter indicates that most of these believers were poor, and some of them were being oppressed by the rich.

Why Did James Write?

Each New Testament letter has its own special theme, purpose, and destination. Paul wrote the Book of Romans to prepare the Roman Christians for his intended visit. First Corinthians was sent to the church at Corinth to help correct certain problems. Galatians was written to a group of churches to warn them against legalism and false teaching.

As you read the Epistle of James, you discover that these Jewish Christians were having some problems in their personal lives and in their church fellowship. For one thing, they were going through difficult testings. They were also facing temptations to sin. Some of the believers were catering to the rich, while others were being robbed by the rich. Church members were competing for offices in the church, particularly teaching offices.

One of the major problems in the church was a failure on the part of many to live what they professed to believe. Furthermore, the tongue was a serious problem, even to the point of creating wars and divisions in the assembly. Worldliness was another problem. Some of the members were disobeying God's Word and were sick physically because of it; and some were straying away from the Lord and the church.

As we review this list of problems, does it appear to be much different from the problems that beset the average local church today? Do we not have in our churches people who are suffering for one reason or another? Do we not have members who talk one way, but walk another way? Is not worldliness a serious problem? Are there not Christians who cannot control their tongues? It seems that James is dealing with very up-to-date matters!

But James was not discussing an array of miscellaneous problems. All of these problems had a common cause: *spiritual immaturity*. These Christians simply were not growing up. This gives us a hint as to the basic theme of this letter: *the marks of maturity in the Christian life*. James used the word *perfect* several times, a word that means "mature, complete" (see 1:4, 17, 25; 2:22; 3:2). By "a perfect man" (3:2) James did not mean a sinless man, but rather one who is mature, balanced, grown-up.

Spiritual maturity is one of the greatest needs in churches today. Too many churches are playpens for babies instead of workshops for adults. The members are not mature enough to eat the solid spiritual food that they need, so they have to be fed on milk (Heb. 5:11-14). Just look at the problems James dealt with and you can see that each of them is characteristic of little children:

> Impatience in difficulties—1:1-4
> Talking but not living the truth—2:14ff
> No control of the tongue—3:1ff
> Fighting and coveting—4:1ff
> Collecting material toys—5:1ff

After over a quarter century of ministry, I am convinced that spiritual immaturity is the number one problem in our churches. God is looking for mature men and women to carry on His work, and sometimes all He can find are little children who cannot even get along with each other.

The five chapters of this Letter suggest the five marks of the mature Christian. If James had made an outline of his letter, based on this theme of maturity, it might look something like this:

Theme: Spiritual Maturity
Key Verse: James 1:4b
The Marks of the Mature Christian:

  I. HE IS PATIENT IN TESTING—chapter 1
    1. Trials on the outside—1:1-12
    2. Temptations on the inside—1:13-27
  II. HE PRACTICES THE TRUTH—
    chapter 2
    1. Faith and love—2:1-13
    2. Faith and works—2:14-26
  III. HE HAS POWER OVER HIS TONGUE
    —chapter 3
    1. Exhortation—3:1-2
    2. Illustrations—3:3-12
      six pictures of the tongue
    3. Application—3:13-18
  IV. HE IS A PEACEMAKER, NOT A
    TROUBLEMAKER— chapter 4
    1. Three wars—4:1-3
    2. Three enemies—4:4-7
    3. Three admonitions—4:8-17
  V. HE IS PRAYERFUL IN TROUBLES—
    chapter 5
    1. Economic troubles—5:1-9
    2. Physical troubles—5:10-16
    3. National troubles—5:17-18
    4. Church troubles—5:19-20

Of course, this is but one approach to this letter; there are other ways to study it. As the chapters are examined, spiritual maturity and how it may be attained will be emphasized.

The Epistle of James logically follows the Epistle to the Hebrews, for one of the major themes of Hebrews is *spiritual perfection*. The word *perfect* is found in Hebrews at least 14 times. The key verse

is Hebrews 6:1—" . . . let us go on unto perfection" meaning, "spiritual maturity." The writer of
Hebrews explained the perfect salvation to be had
in Christ. James exhorted his readers to build on
this perfect salvation and grow into maturity. Without the perfect work of Christ there could be no
perfecting of the believers.

How Can We Get the Most out of this Study?
Since the theme is spiritual maturity, we must begin
by examining our own hearts to see where we are
in the Christian life.

First of all, it is essential that we have been born
again. Apart from spiritual birth there can be no
spiritual maturity. James mentioned the new birth
early in his letter: "Of His own will begat He us
with the word of truth" (James 1:18). The parallel
to this is 1 Peter 1:23—"Being born again, not of
corruptible seed, but of incorruptible, by the Word
of God, which liveth and abideth forever."

Just as a human baby has two parents, so a spiritual baby has two parents—the Word of God and
the Spirit of God. We have already quoted two
verses that mention the Word of God. John 3:5-6
mentions the Spirit of God. (It is my conviction that
"born of water" here refers to physical birth. All
babies are "born of water." Nicodemus thought in
terms of physical birth in John 3:5.)

How, then, is a person "born again"? The Spirit
of God takes the Word of God and generates new
life within the heart of the sinner who believes on
Jesus Christ. It is a miracle. The Spirit uses the
Word to convict the sinner, and then to reveal the
Saviour. We are saved by faith (Eph. 2:8-9) and
faith comes from the Word of God (Rom. 10:17).

If we have been born again, there is a second

essential for getting the most out of what James has written: we must honestly examine our lives in the light of God's Word. James compares the Bible to a mirror (James 1:22ff). As we study the Word, we are looking into the divine mirror and seeing ourselves as we really are. But James warns us that we must be honest about what we see and not merely glance at the image and walk away.

Perhaps you heard about the primitive savage who looked into a mirror for the first time. He was so shocked at what he saw that he broke the mirror! Many Christians make the same mistake: they criticize the preacher or the lesson, when they ought to be judging themselves.

This leads to a third essential: we must obey what God teaches us, no matter what the cost. We must be "doers of the word and not hearers only" (James 1:22). It is easy to attend a Bible study, share the lesson, and discuss it; but it is much more difficult to go out into life in the workaday world and practice what we have learned. The blessing does not come in *studying* the Word, but in *doing* the Word. Unless we are willing to obey, the Lord is not obligated to teach us (John 7:17).

The fourth essential is that we be prepared for some extra trials and testings. Whenever we are serious about spiritual growth, the Enemy gets serious about opposing us. Perhaps you feel a need for more patience. Then be prepared for more trials, because "tribulation worketh patience" (Rom. 5:3). The real examinations in Bible study come in the school of life, not in the classroom.

I read recently about a man who was burdened to grow in his patience. He knew he was immature in that area of his life, and he wanted to grow up. He sincerely prayed, "Lord, help me to grow in patience. I want to have more self-control in this area of my life." That morning, he missed his train to work and spent the next 50 minutes pacing the platform and complaining of his plight. As the next train to the city arrived, the man realized how stupid he had been. "The Lord gave me nearly an hour to grow in my patience, and all I did was practice my impatience!" he said to himself.

There may come a time in this study when you may decide that continuing is too dangerous. Satan may turn on the heat and make things so difficult for you that you will want to retreat. *Don't do it!* When that time arrives, you will be on the verge of a new and wonderful blessing in your own life, a thrilling new step of maturity. Even if Satan does turn on the heat, your Father in heaven keeps His almighty hand on the thermostat!

Even physical maturity is not always an easy, pleasant experience. The teenager walking that difficult bridge from childhood to adulthood has his frustrations and failures; but if he keeps on going (and growing), he eventually enters a wonderful life of maturity. Christian growth is not automatic, as is physical growth. Christian maturity is something we must work at constantly. So, don't give up! There is travail in birth, and there is also travail in maturity (Gal. 4:19).

Finally, we must measure our spiritual growth by the Word of God. We should not measure ourselves by other Christians, but by the Word of God and the Son of God (Eph. 4:13). At the close of this book, a dozen questions are listed based on James, that may help in a personal evaluation. Feel free to turn to them at any time, because regular examinations are good for spiritual health.

Not everyone who grows old, grows up. There is

a difference between age and maturity. Just because a Christian has been saved for 10 or 20 years does not guarantee that he is mature in the Lord. Mature Christians are happy Christians, useful Christians, Christians who help to encourage others and to build their local church. As we study James together, with God's help we will learn together and mature together.

2

Turning Trials into Triumphs

(JAMES 1:2–12)

Perhaps you have seen the bumper sticker that reads: "When life hands you a lemon, make lemonade!" It is easier to smile at that statement than to practice it, but the basic philosophy is sound. In fact, it is biblical. Throughout the Bible are people who turned defeat into victory and trial into triumph. Instead of being victims, they became victors.

James tells us that we can have this same experience today. No matter what the trials may be on the outside (1:1-12) or the temptations on the inside (1:13-27), through faith in Christ we can experience victory. The result of this victory is spiritual maturity.

If we are going to turn trials into triumphs, we must obey four imperatives: *count* (1:2), *know* (1:3), *let* (1:4 and 9-11), and *ask* (1:5-8). Or, to put it another way, there are four essentials for victory in trials: a joyful attitude, an understanding mind, a surrendered will, and a heart that wants to believe.

Count—a Joyful Attitude (1:2)

Outlook determines outcome, and attitude determines action. God tells us to *expect trials*. It is not "*if* you fall into various testings" but "when you fall into various testings." The believer who expects his Christian life to be easy is in for a shock. Jesus warned His disciples, "In the world ye shall have tribulation" (John 16:33). Paul told his converts that "we must through much tribulation enter into the kingdom of God" (Acts 14:22).

Because we are God's "scattered people" and not God's "sheltered people," we must experience trials. We cannot always expect everything to go our way. Some trials come simply because we are human— sickness, accidents, disappointments, even seeming tragedies. Other trials come because we are Christians. Peter emphasizes this in his first letter: "Beloved, think it not strange concerning the fiery trial which is to try you, as though some strange thing happened unto you" (1 Peter 4:12). Satan fights us, the world opposes us, and this makes for a life of battle.

The phrase "fall into" does not suggest a stupid accident. Translate it "encounter, come across." A Christian certainly should not manufacture trials. The Greek word translated "divers" means "various, varicolored." Peter uses the same word in 1 Peter 1:6—"Ye are in heaviness through manifold temptations." The trials of life are not all alike; they are like variegated yarn that the weaver uses to make a beautiful rug. God arranges and mixes the colors and experiences of life. The final product is a beautiful thing for His glory.

My wife and I once visited a world-famous weaver and watched his men and women work on the looms. I noticed that the undersides of the rugs were not very beautiful: the patterns were obscure and the loose ends of yarn dangled, "Don't judge the worker or the work by looking at the wrong side," our guide told us. In the same way, we are looking at the wrong side of life; only the Lord sees the finished pattern. Let's not judge Him or His work from what we see today. His work is not finished yet!

The key word is count. It is a financial term, and it means "to evaluate." Paul used it several times in Philippians 3. When Paul became a Christian, he evaluated his life and set new goals and priorities. Things that were once important to him became "garbage" in the light of his experience with Christ. When we face the trials of life, we must evaluate them in the light of what God is doing for us.

This explains why the dedicated Christian can have joy in the midst of trials: *he lives for the things that matter most*. Even our Lord was able to endure the Cross because of "the joy that was set before Him" (Heb. 12:2), the joy of returning to heaven and sharing His glory with His church.

Our values determine our evaluations. If we value comfort more than character, then trials will upset us. If we value the material and physical more than the spiritual, we will not be able to "count it all joy." If we live only for the present and forget the future, then trials will make us bitter, not better. Job had the right outlook when he said, "But He knoweth the way that I take: when He hath tried me, I shall come forth as gold" (Job 23:10).

So, when trials come, immediately give thanks to

the Lord and adopt a joyful attitude. Do not pretend; do not try self-hypnosis; simply look at trials through the eyes of faith. Outlook determines outcome; to *end* with joy, *begin* with joy.

"But how," we may ask, "is it possible to rejoice in the midst of trials?" The second imperative explains this.

Know—an Understanding Mind (1:3)

What do Christians know that makes it easier to face trials and benefit from them?

1. *Faith is always tested.* When God called Abraham to live by faith, He tested him in order to increase his faith. God always tests us to bring out the *best;* Satan tempts us to bring out the worst. The testing of our faith proves that we are truly born again.

2. *Testing works for us, not against us.* The word *trying* can be translated "approval." Again, Peter helps us understand it better: "That the trial of your faith, being much more precious than of gold that perisheth . . . (1 Peter 1:7). A gold prospector brings his ore sample into the assayer's office to be tested. The sample itself may not be worth more than a few dollars, but the *approval*—the official statement about the ore—is worth millions! It assures the prospector that he has a gold mine. God's approval of our faith is precious, because it assures us that our faith is genuine.

Trials work *for* the believer, not against him. Paul said, "And we know that all things work together for good" (Rom. 8:28); and, "For our light affliction, which is but for a moment, worketh for us a far more exceeding and eternal weight of glory" (2 Cor. 4:17).

3. *Trials rightly used help us to mature.* What

does God want to produce in our lives? Patience, endurance, and the ability to keep going when things are tough. "We glory in tribulations also: knowing that tribulation worketh patience; and patience, experience; and experience, hope" (Rom. 5:3-4). In the Bible, *patience* is not a passive acceptance of circumstances. It is a courageous perseverance in the face of suffering and difficulty.

Immature people are always impatient; mature people are patient and persistent. Impatience and unbelief usually go together, just as faith and patience do. "Be . . . followers of them who through faith and patience inherit the promises" (Heb. 6:12). "For ye have need of patience, that, after ye have done the will of God, ye might receive the promise" (Heb. 10:36). "He that believeth shall not make haste" (Isa. 28:16.)

God wants to make us patient because that is the key to every other blessing. The little child who does not learn patience will not learn much of anything else. When the believer learns to wait on the Lord, then God can do great things for him. Abraham ran ahead of the Lord, married Hagar, and brought great sorrow into his home (Gen. 16). Moses ran ahead of God, murdered a man, and had to spend 40 years with the sheep to learn patience (Ex. 2:11ff). Peter almost killed a man in his impatience (John 18:10-11).

The only way the Lord can develop patience and character in our lives is through trials. Endurance cannot be attained by reading a book (even this one), listening to a sermon, or even praying a prayer. We must go through the difficulties of life, trust God, and obey Him. The result will be patience and character. Knowing this, we can face trials joyfully. We know what trials will do in us

and for us, and we know that the end result will
bring glory to God.

This fact explains why studying the Bible helps
us grow in patience (Rom. 15:4). As we read about
Abraham, Joseph, Moses, David, and even our
Lord, we realize that God has a purpose in trials.
God fulfills His purposes as we trust Him. There is
no substitute for an understanding mind. Satan can
defeat the ignorant believer, but he cannot overcome the Christian who knows his Bible and understands the purposes of God.

Let—a Surrendered Will (1:4, 9-11)

God cannot build our character without our coop-
eration. If we resist Him, then He chastens us into
submission. But if we submit to Him, then He can
accomplish His work. He is not satisfied with a
halfway job. God wants a perfect work; He wants
a finished product that is mature and complete.

God's goal for our lives is maturity. It would be a
tragedy if our children remained little babies. We
enjoy watching them mature, even though maturity
brings dangers as well as delights. Many Christians
shelter themselves from the trials of life, and as a
result, never grow up. God wants the "little children" to become "young men," and the "young
men" He wants to become "fathers" (1 John
2:12-14).

Paul outlined three works that are involved in a
complete Christian life (Eph. 2:8-10). First, there is
the work God does *for us*, which is salvation. Jesus
Christ completed this work on the cross. If we trust
Him, He will save us. Second, there is the work
God does *in us*; "For we are His workmanship."
This work is known as *sanctification*: God builds
our character and we become more like Jesus

Christ, "conformed to the image of His Son" (Rom.
8:29). The third work is what God does *through
us*—service. We are "created in Christ Jesus unto
good works."

God builds character before He calls to service.
He must work *in* us before He can work *through*
us. God spent 25 years working in Abraham before
He could give him his promised son. God worked
13 years in Joseph's life, putting him into "various
testings" before He could put him on the throne of
Egypt. He spent 80 years preparing Moses for 40
years of service. Our Lord took three years training
His disciples, building their character.

But God cannot work in us without our consent.
There must be a surrendered will. The mature person does not argue with God's will; instead, he accepts it willingly and obeys it joyfully. "Doing the
will of God from the heart" (Eph. 6:6). If we try to
go through trials without surrendered wills, we will
end up more like immature children than mature
adults.

Jonah is an illustration of this. God commanded
Jonah to preach to the Gentiles at Nineveh, and he
refused. God chastened Jonah before the prophet
accepted his commission. But Jonah did not obey
God from the heart. He did not grow in this experience. How do we know? Because in the last chapter
of Jonah, the prophet is acting like a spoiled child!
He is sitting outside the city pouting, hoping that
God will send judgment. He is impatient with the
sun, the wind, the gourd, the worm, and with God.

One difficult stage of maturing is *weaning*. A
child being weaned is sure that his mother no
longer loves him and that everything is against him.
Actually, weaning is a step toward maturity and
liberty. It is good for the child! Sometimes God has

to wean His children away from their childish toys
and immature attitudes. David pictured this in
Psalm 131: "Surely I have behaved and quieted myself, as a child that is weaned of his mother: my
soul is even as a weaned child" (v. 2). God uses
trials to wean us away from childish things; but if
we do not surrender to Him, we will become even
more immature.

In verses 9-11, James applies this principle to two
different kinds of Christians: the poor and the rich.
Apparently, money and social status were real
problems among these people (see 2:1-7 and 15-16;
4:1-3 and 13-17; 5:1-8). *God's testings have a way of
leveling us.* When testing comes to the poor man,
he lets God have his way and rejoices that he possesses spiritual riches that cannot be taken from
him. When testing comes to the rich man, he also
lets God have His way, and he rejoices that his
riches in Christ cannot wither or fade away. In
other words, it is not your material resources that
take you through the testings of life; it is your spiritual resources.

We have three imperatives from James so far:
count—a joyful attitude; *know*—an understanding
heart; *let*—a surrendered will. He gives a fourth.

Ask—a believing heart (1:5-8)

The people to whom James wrote had problems
with their praying (4:1-3 and 5:13-18). When we
are going through God-ordained difficulties, what
should we pray about? James gives the answer: ask
God for *wisdom.*

James has a great deal to say about wisdom (1:5;
3:13-18). The Jewish people were lovers of wisdom,
as the Book of Proverbs gives evidence. Someone
has said that knowledge is the ability to take things

apart, while wisdom is the ability to put them together. Wisdom is the right use of knowledge. All
of us know people who are educated fools: they
have brilliant academic records, but they cannot
make the simplest decisions in life. I once met a
gifted professor on a seminary campus, and he was
wearing two hats!

Why do we need wisdom when we are going
through trials? Why not ask for strength, or grace,
or even deliverance? For this reason: *we need wisdom so we will not waste the opportunities God is
giving us to mature.* Wisdom helps us understand
how to use these circumstances for our good and
God's glory.

An associate of mine, a gifted secretary, was going through great trials. She had had a stroke, her
husband had gone blind, and then he had to be
taken to the hospital where (we were sure) he
would die. I saw her in church one Sunday and assured her that I was praying for her.

"What are you asking God to do?" she asked,
and her question startled me.

"I'm asking God to help you and strengthen
you," I replied.

"I appreciate that," she said, "but pray about one
more thing. Pray that I'll have the wisdom not to
waste all of this!"

She knew the meaning of James 1:5.

James not only explained *what* to ask for (wisdom), but he also described *how* to ask. We are to
ask in faith. We do not have to be afraid, for God
is anxious to answer, and He will never scold us!
"He giveth more grace" (James 4:6). He also gives
more and more wisdom. The greatest enemy to answered prayer is unbelief.

James compares the doubting believer to the

waves of the sea, up one minute and down the next. While vacationing in Hawaii, I learned that you cannot trust the waves. I was sitting on a rock by the ocean, watching the waves and enjoying the sunshine. I heard a sound behind me, turned to see who was approaching, and instantly was drenched by a huge wave! Never turn your back on the waves—they are down, then they are up.

This is the experience of the "double-minded man." Faith says, "Yes!" but unbelief says, "No!" Then doubt comes along and says "Yes!" one minute and "No!" the next. It was doubt that made Peter sink in the waves as he was walking to Jesus (Matt. 14:22-33). Jesus asked him, "O thou of little faith, wherefore didst thou doubt?" When Peter started his walk of faith, he kept his eyes on Christ. But when he was distracted by the wind and waves, he ceased to walk by faith; and he began to sink. He was double-minded, and he almost drowned.

Many Christians live like corks on the waves: up one minute, down the next; tossed back and forth. This kind of experience is evidence of immaturity. Paul used a similar idea in Ephesians 4:14—"That we henceforth be no more children, tossed to and fro, and carried about with every wind of doctrine, by the sleight of men, and cunning craftiness, whereby they lie in wait to deceive." If we have believing and united hearts, we can ask in faith and God will give the wisdom we need. Instability and immaturity go together.

James closed this session with a beatitude: "Blessed is the man that endureth temptation" (1:12). He started (v. 2) and ended with joy. Outlook determines outcome. This beatitude is a great encouragement because it promises a crown to those who patiently endure trials. Paul often used athletic illustrations in his letters, and James does so here. He is not saying that the sinner is saved by enduring trials. He is saying that the believer is rewarded by enduring trials.

How is he rewarded? First, by growth in Christian character. This is more important than anything else. He is rewarded also by bringing glory to God and by being granted a crown of life when Jesus Christ returns. First the cross, then the crown. First the suffering, then the glory. God does not help us by removing the tests, but by making the tests work for us. Satan wants to use the tests to tear us down, but God uses them to build us up.

In verse 12, James used a very important word, *love*. We would expect him to write, "the crown of life, which the Lord hath promised to them that trust Him" or "that obey Him." Why did James use *love?* Because love is the spiritual motivation behind every imperative in this section.

Why do we have a joyful attitude as we face trials? Because we love God, and He loves us, and He will not harm us. Why do we have an understanding mind? Because He loves us and has shared His truth with us, and we love Him in return. Why do we have a surrendered will? Because we love Him. Where there is love, there is surrender and obedience. Why do we have a believing heart? Because love and faith go together. When you love someone, you trust him, and you do not hesitate to ask him for help.

Love is the spiritual force behind the imperatives James gives us. If we love God, we will have no problem counting, knowing, letting, and asking. But there is another factor involved: love keeps us faithful to the Lord. The double-minded person (1:8) is like an unfaithful husband or wife: he wants to love both God and the world. James admonished, "Purify your hearts, ye double-minded!" (4:8) The Greek word translated *purify* literally means "make chaste." The picture is that of an unfaithful lover.

Let's go back to the weaning. The child who loves his mother, and who is sure that his mother loves him, will be able to get through the weaning and start to grow up. The Christian who loves God, and who knows that God loves him, will not fall apart when God permits trials to come. *He is secure in God's love.* He is not double-minded, trying to love both God and the world. Lot was double-minded; when trials came, he failed miserably. Abraham was the friend of God; he loved God and trusted Him. When trials came, Abraham triumphed and matured in the faith.

God's purpose in trials is maturity. "Let patience have her perfect work, that ye may be perfect and entire, wanting nothing." The Charles B. Williams translation says it graphically: "But you must let your endurance come to its perfect product so that you may be fully developed and perfectly equipped."

If that is what you want, then in love to Christ, count, know, let, and ask.

3

How to Handle Temptation

(JAMES 1:13–18)

The mature person is patient in trials. Sometimes the trials are testings on the outside, and sometimes they are temptations on the inside. Trials may be tests sent by God, or they may be temptations sent by Satan and encouraged by our own fallen nature. It is this second aspect of trials—temptations on the inside—that James dealt with in this section.

We may ask, "Why did James connect the two? What is the relationship between testings without and temptations within?" Simply this: if we are not careful, the testings on the outside may become temptations on the inside. When our circumstances are difficult, we may find ourselves complaining against God, questioning His love, and resisting His will. At this point, Satan provides us with an opportunity to escape the difficulty. This opportunity is a temptation.

There are many illustrations of this truth found in the Bible. Abraham arrived in Canaan and dis-

31

covered a famine there. He was not able to care for his flocks and herds. This trial was an opportunity to prove God; but Abraham turned it into a temptation and went down to Egypt. God had to chasten Abraham to bring him back to the place of obedience and blessing.

While Israel was wandering in the wilderness, the nation often turned testings into temptations and tempted the Lord. No sooner had they been delivered from Egypt than their water supply vanished and they had to march for three days without water. When they did find water, it was so bitter they could not drink it. Immediately they began to murmur and blame God. They turned their testing into a temptation, and they failed.

Certainly, God does not want us to yield to temptation, yet neither can He spare us the experience of temptation. We are not God's *sheltered* people; we are God's *scattered* people. If we are to mature, we must face testings and temptations. There are three facts that we must consider if we are to overcome temptation.

Consider God's Judgment (1:13-16)

This is a negative approach, but it is an important one. James said, "Look ahead and see where sin ends—death!" Do not blame God for temptation. He is too holy to be tempted, and He is too loving to tempt others. God does test us, as He did Abraham (Gen. 22); but He does not and cannot tempt us. It is we who turn occasions of testing into temptations.

A temptation is an opportunity to accomplish a good thing in a bad way, out of the will of God. Is it wrong to want to pass an examination? Of course not; but if you cheat to pass it, then you have sinned. The temptation to cheat is an opportunity to accomplish a good thing (passing the examination) in a bad way. It is not wrong to eat; but if you consider stealing the food, you are tempting yourself.

We think of sin as a single act, but God sees it as a process. Adam committed one act of sin, and yet that one act brought sin, death, and judgment upon the whole human race. James described this process of sin in four stages.

Desire (1:14). The word *lust* means any kind of desire, and not necessarily sexual passions. The normal desires of life were given to us by God and, of themselves, are not sinful. Without these desires, we could not function. Unless we felt hunger and thirst, we would never eat and drink, and we would die. Without fatigue, the body would never rest and would eventually wear out. Sex is a normal desire; without it the human race could not continue.

It is when we want to satisfy these desires in ways outside God's will that we get into trouble. Eating is normal; gluttony is sin. Sleep is normal; laziness is sin. "Marriage is honorable in all, and the bed undefiled; but whoremongers and adulterers God will judge" (Heb. 13:4).

Some people try to become "spiritual" by denying these normal desires, or by seeking to suppress them; but this only makes them less than human. These fundamental desires of life are the steam in the boiler that makes the machinery go. Turn off the steam and you have no power. Let the steam go its own way and you have destruction. The secret is in *constant control*. These desires must be our servants and not our masters; and this we can do through Jesus Christ.

Deception (1:14). No temptation appears as temptation; it always seems more alluring than it really is. James used two illustrations from the world of sports to prove his point. *Drawn away* carries with it the idea of the baiting of a trap; and *enticed* in the original Greek means "to bait a hook." The hunter and the fisherman have to use bait to attract and catch their prey. No animal is deliberately going to step into a trap and no fish will knowingly bite at a naked hook. The idea is to *hide* the trap and the hook.

Temptation always carries with it some bait that appeals to our natural desires. The bait not only attracts us, but it also hides the fact that yielding to the desire will eventually bring sorrow and punishment. It is the bait that is the exciting thing. Lot would never have moved toward Sodom had he not seen the "well-watered plains of Jordan" (Gen. 13:10ff). When David looked upon his neighbor's wife, he would never have committed adultery had he seen the tragic consequences: the death of a baby (Bathsheba's son), the murder of a brave soldier (Uriah), the violation of a daughter (Tamas). *The bait keeps us from seeing the consequences of sin.*

When Jesus was tempted by Satan, He always dealt with the temptation on the basis of the Word of God. Three times He said, "It is written." From the human point of view, turning stones into bread to satisfy hunger is a sensible thing to do; but not from God's point of view. When you know the Bible, you can detect the bait and deal with it decisively. This is what it means to walk by faith and not by sight.

Disobedience (1:15). We have moved from the *emotions* (desire) and the *intellect* (deception) to the *will*. James changed the picture from hunting and fishing to the birth of a baby. Desire conceives a method for taking the bait. The will approves and acts; and the result is sin. Whether we feel it or not, we are hooked and trapped. The baby is born, and just wait until it matures!

Christian living is a matter of the will, not the feelings. I often hear believers say, "I don't feel like reading the Bible." Or, "I don't feel like attending prayer meeting." Children operate on the basis of feeling, but adults operate on the basis of will. *They act because it is right, no matter how they feel.* This explains why immature Christians easily fall into temptation: they let their feelings make the decisions. The more you exercise your will in saying a decisive "No" to temptation, the more God will take control of your life. "For it is God which worketh in you both to will and to do of His good pleasure" (Phil. 2:13).

Death (1:15). Disobedience gives birth to death, not life. It may take years for the sin to mature, but when it does, the result will be death. If we will only believe God's Word and see this final tragedy, it will encourage us not to yield to temptation. God has erected this barrier because He loves us. "Have I any pleasure at all that the wicked should die?" (Ezek. 18:23)

These four stages in temptation and sin are perfectly depicted in the first sin recorded in the Bible in Genesis 3.

The serpent used *desire* to interest Eve: "For God doth know that in the day ye eat thereof, then your eyes shall be opened, and ye shall be as gods, knowing good and evil" (Gen. 3:5). Is there anything wrong with gaining knowledge? Is there anything wrong with eating food? Eve saw that "the tree was good for food" (Gen. 3:6), and her desire was aroused.

Paul described the deception of Eve in 2 Corinthians 11:3. "But I fear, lest by any means, as the serpent beguiled Eve through his subtilty, so your minds should be corrupted from the simplicity that is in Christ." Satan is the deceiver, and he seeks to deceive the mind. The bait that he used with Eve was the fact that the forbidden tree was good and pleasant, and that eating of it would make her wise. She saw the bait but forgot the Lord's warning: "In the day that thou eatest thereof thou shalt surely die" (Gen. 2:17).

Eve disobeyed God by taking the fruit of the tree and eating it. Then she shared it with her husband, and he disobeyed God. Because Adam was not deceived, but sinned with his eyes wide open, it is his sin that plunged the human race into tragedy. (Read 1 Tim. 2:12-15 and Rom. 5:12-21.)

Both Adam and Eve experienced immediate spiritual death (separation from God), and ultimate physical death. All men die because of Adam (1 Cor. 15:21-22). The person who dies without Jesus Christ will experience eternal death, the lake of fire (Rev. 20:11-15).

Whenever you are faced with temptation, get your eyes off the bait and look ahead to see the consequences of sin: *the judgment of God*. "For the wages of sin is death" (Rom. 6:23).

Consider God's Goodness (1:17)

One of the enemy's tricks is to convince us that our Father is holding out on us, that He does not really love us and care for us. When Satan approached Eve, he suggested that if God really loved her, He would permit her to eat of the forbidden tree.

When Satan tempted Jesus, he raised the question of hunger. "If your Father loves You, why are You hungry?"

The goodness of God is a great barrier against yielding to temptation. Since God is good, we do not need any other person (including Satan) to meet our needs. It is better to be hungry *in* the will of God than full *outside* the will of God. Once we start to doubt God's goodness, we will be attracted to Satan's offers; and the natural desires within will reach out for his bait. Moses warned Israel not to forget God's goodness when they began to enjoy the blessings of the Promised Land (Deut. 6:10-15). We need this warning today.

James presented four facts about the goodness of God.

God gives only good gifts. Everything good in this world comes from God. If it did not come from God, it is not good. If it comes from God, it must be good, even if we do not see the goodness in it immediately. Paul's thorn in the flesh was given to him by God and it seemed to be a strange gift; yet it became a tremendous blessing to him (2 Cor. 12:1-10).

The way God gives is good. We can translate the second clause "and every act of giving." It is possible for someone to give us a gift in a manner that is less than loving. The value of a gift can be diminished by the way it is given to us. But when God gives us a blessing, He does it in a loving, gracious manner. *What* He gives and *how* He gives are both good.

He gives constantly. "Cometh down" is a present participle: "it keeps on coming down." God does not give occasionally; He gives constantly. Even when we do not see His gifts, He is sending them.

How do we know this? Because He tells us so and
we believe His Word.

God does not change. There are no shadows with
the Father of Lights. It is impossible for God to
change. He cannot change for the worse because
He is holy; He cannot change for the better because He is already perfect. The light of the sun
varies as the earth changes, but the sun itself is still
shining. If shadows come between us and the
Father, He did not cause them. He is the unchang-
ing God. This means that we should never question
His love or doubt His goodness when difficulties
come or temptations appear.

If King David had remembered the goodness of
the Lord, he would not have taken Bathsheba and
committed those terrible sins. At least this is what
Nathan the prophet told the king. "Thus saith the
Lord God of Israel, 'I anointed thee king over
Israel, and I delivered thee out of the hand of Saul;
and I gave thee thy master's house, and thy master's
wives into thy bosom, and gave thee the house of
Israel and of Judah; and if that had been too little,
I would moreover have given unto thee such and
such things'" (2 Sam. 12:7-8). Note the repetition
of the word *give* in this brief statement. God had
been good to David, yet David forgot God's goodness and took the bait.

The first barrier against temptation is a negative
one: the judgment of God. This second barrier is
positive: the goodness of God. A fear of God is a
healthy attitude, but the love of God must balance
it. We can obey Him because He may chasten us;
or we can obey Him because He has already been
so generous to us, and because we love Him for it.

It was this positive attitude that helped to keep
Joseph from sinning when he was tempted by his

master's wife (Gen. 39:7ff). "Behold, with me around, my master does not concern himself with anything in the house, and he has put all that he owns in my charge. There is no one greater in this house than I, and he has withheld nothing from me except you, because you are his wife. How then could I do this great evil, and sin against God?" (Gen. 39:8-9, NASB) Joseph knew that all these blessings had come from God. It was the goodness of God, through the hands of his employer, that restrained him in the hour of temptation.

God's gifts are always better than Satan's bargains. Satan never gives any gifts, because you end up *paying for them dearly*. "It is the blessing of the Lord that makes rich, and He adds no sorrow to it" (Prov. 10:22, NASB). Achan forgot the warning of God and the goodness of God, saw the forbidden wealth, coveted it, and took it. He became rich, but the sorrow that followed turned his riches into poverty (Josh. 7).

The next time you are tempted, meditate on the goodness of God in your life. If you think you need something, wait on the Lord to provide it. Never toy with the devil's bait. One purpose for temptation is to teach us patience. David was tempted twice to kill King Saul and hasten his own coronation, but he resisted the temptation and waited for God's time.

Consider God's Divine Nature Within (1:18)

In the first barrier, God says, "Look ahead and beware of judgment." In the second barrier, He says, "Look around and see how good I have been to you." But with this third barrier, God says, "Look within and realize that you have been born from above and possess the divine nature."

James used birth as a picture of desire leading to sin and death (1:15). He also used it to explain how we can enjoy victory over temptation and sin. The Apostle John used a similar approach in 1 John 3:9, where "his seed" refers to the divine life and nature within the believer. Note the characteristics of this birth.

It is divine. Nicodemus thought he had to reenter his mother's womb to be born again, but he was wrong. This birth is not of the flesh: it is from above (John 3:1-7). It is the work of God. Just as we did not generate our own human birth, we cannot generate our own spiritual birth. When we put our faith in Jesus Christ, it was God who performed the miracle.

It is gracious. We did not earn it or deserve it; God gave us spiritual birth because of His own grace and will. "Which were born, not of blood [human descent], nor of the will of the flesh [human efforts], nor of the will of man [human assistance], but of God" (John 1:13). No one can be born again because of his relatives, his resolutions, or his religion. The new birth is the work of God.

It is through God's Word. Just as human birth requires two parents, so divine birth has two parents: the Word of God and the Spirit of God. "That which is born of the flesh is flesh; and that which is born of the Spirit is spirit" (John 3:6). "Being born again, not of corruptible seed, but of incorruptible, by the Word of God, which liveth and abideth forever" (1 Peter 1:23). The Spirit of God uses the Word of God to bring about the miracle of the new birth. Since the Word of God is "living and powerful" (Heb. 4:12) it can generate life in the heart of the sinner who trusts Christ; and that life is God's life.

It is the finest birth possible. We are "a kind of firstfruits of His creatures" James wrote to Jewish believers, and the word *firstfruits* would be meaningful to them. The Old Testament Jews brought the firstfruits to the Lord as the expression of their devotion and obedience. "Honor the Lord with thy substance, and with the firstfruits of all thine increase" (Prov. 3:9). Of all the creatures God has in this universe, Christians are the very highest and the finest! We share God's nature. For this reason, it is beneath our dignity to accept Satan's bait or to desire sinful things. A higher birth must mean a higher life.

By granting us a new birth, God declares that He cannot accept the old birth. Throughout the Bible, God rejects the firstborn and accepts the secondborn. He accepted Abel, not Cain; Isaac, not Ishmael; Jacob, not Esau. He rejects your first birth (no matter how noble it might have been in the eyes of men), and He announces that you need a second birth.

It is this experience of the new birth that helps us overcome temptation. If we let the old nature (from the first birth) take over, we will fail. We received our old nature (the flesh) from Adam, and he was a failure. But if we yield to the new nature, we will succeed; for that new nature comes from Christ, and He is the Victor.

A Sunday School child explained the matter in simple terms. "Two men live in my heart: the old Adam and Jesus. When temptation knocks at the door, somebody has to answer. If I let Adam answer, I will sin; *so I send Jesus to answer.* He always wins!"

Of course, this new nature must be fed the Word of God daily, that it might be strong to fight the battle. Just as the Holy Spirit used the Word of God to give you spiritual birth, He uses the Word to give you spiritual strength. "Man shall not live by bread alone, but by every word that proceedeth out of the mouth of God" (Matt. 4:4).

No matter what excuses we make, we have no one to blame for sin but ourselves. Our own desires lead us into temptation and sin. God is not to blame. But God has erected these three barriers to keep us from sin. If we heed the barriers, we will win a crown (1:12). If we break through the barriers, we will find a coffin (1:15). Which will it be?

4

Stop Kidding Yourself

(JAMES 1:19–27)

The emphasis in this section is on the dangers of self-deception: "deceiving your own selves" (v. 22); "deceiveth his own heart" (v. 26). If a Christian sins because Satan deceives him, that is one thing. But if he deceives himself, that is a far more serious matter.

Many people are deceiving themselves into thinking they are saved when they are not. "Many will say to me in that day, 'Lord, Lord, have we not prophesied in Thy name? and in Thy name have cast out devils? and in Thy name done many wonderful works?' And then will I profess unto them, 'I never knew you: depart from Me, ye that work iniquity'" (Matt. 7:22-23).

But there are true believers who are fooling themselves concerning their Christian walk. They think they are spiritual when they are not. It is a mark of maturity when a person faces himself honestly, knows himself, and admits his needs. It

43

is the immature person who pretends, "I am rich, and increased with goods, and have need of nothing" (Rev. 3:17).

Spiritual reality results from the proper relationship to God through His Word. God's Word is truth (John 17:17), and if we are rightly related to God's truth, we cannot be dishonest or hypocritical. In these verses, James stated that we have three responsibilities toward God's Word; and if we fulfill these responsibilities, we will have an honest walk with God and men.

Receive the Word (1:19-21)

James calls God's Word "the engrafted word" (v. 21), which means "the implanted word." Borrowing from our Lord's Parable of the Sower (Matt. 13:1-9 and 18-23), he compares God's Word to seed and the human heart to soil. In His parable, Jesus described four kinds of hearts: *the hard heart*, which did not understand or receive the Word and therefore bore no fruit; *the shallow heart*, which was very emotional but had no depth, and bore no fruit; *the crowded heart*, which lacked repentance and permitted sin to crowd out the Word; and *the fruitful heart*, which received the Word, allowed it to take root, and produced a bountiful harvest of fruit.

The final test of salvation is fruit. This means a changed life, Christian character and conduct, and ministry to others in the glory of God. This fruit might be winning souls to Christ (Rom. 1:16), growing in holy living (Rom. 6:22), sharing our material possessions (Rom. 15:28), spiritual character (Gal. 5:22-23), good works (Col. 1:10), and even praising the Lord (Heb. 13:15). Religious works may be manufactured, but they do not have

STOP KIDDING YOURSELF   45

life in them, nor do they bring glory to God. Real
fruit has in it the seed for more fruit, so that the
harvest continues to grow fruit, more fruit, much
fruit (John 15:1-5).

But the Word of God cannot work in our lives
unless we receive it in the right way. Jesus not
only said "Take heed what ye hear" (Mark 4:24)
but He also said, "Take heed how ye hear" (Luke
8:18). Too many people are in that tragic condition
in which "hearing they hear not, neither do they
understand" (Matt. 13:13). They attend Bible
classes and church services but never seem to grow.
Is it the fault of the teacher or the preacher?
Perhaps, but it may also be the fault of the hearer.
It is possible to be "dull of hearing" (Heb. 5:11)
because of decay of the spiritual life.

If the seed of the Word is to be planted in our
hearts, then we must obey the instructions James
gives us.

Swift to hear (1:19). "Who hath ears to hear, let
him hear!" (Matt. 13:9) "So then faith cometh by
hearing, and hearing by the Word of God" (Rom.
10:17). Just as the servant is quick to hear his
master's voice, and the mother to hear her baby's
smallest cry, so the believer should be quick to
hear what God has to say.

There is a beautiful illustration of this truth in
the life of King David (2 Sam. 23:14-17). David
was hiding from the Philistines who were in posses-
sion of Bethlehem. He yearned for a drink of the
cool water from the well in Bethlehem, a well that
he had often visited in his boyhood and youth. He
did not issue an order to his men; he simply said
to himself, "Oh, that one would give me drink of
the water of the well of Bethlehem, which is by
the gate" (2 Sam. 23:15). Three of his mighty men

heard their king sigh for the water, and they risked their lives to secure the water and bring it to him. They were "swift to hear."

Slow to speak (1:19). We have two ears and one mouth, which ought to remind us to listen more than we speak. Too many times we argue with God's Word, if not audibly, at least in our hearts and minds. "He that refraineth his lips is wise" (Prov. 10:19b). "He that hath knowledge spareth his words" (Prov. 17:27a). Instead of being slow to speak, the lawyer in Luke 10:29 argued with Jesus by asking, "And who is my neighbor?" In the early church, the services were informal; and often the listeners would debate with the speaker. There were even fightings and wars among the brethren James was writing to (James 4:1).

Slow to wrath (1:19). Do not get angry at God or His Word. "He that is slow to wrath is of great understanding: but he that is hasty of spirit exalteth folly" (Prov. 14:29). When the prophet Nathan told King David the story about "the stolen ewe lamb," the king became angry, but at the wrong person. "Thou art the man" said Nathan, and David then confessed, "I have sinned" (2 Sam. 12). In the garden, Peter was slow to hear, swift to speak, and swift to anger—and he almost killed a man with the sword. Many church fights are the result of short tempers and hasty words. There is a godly anger against sin (Eph. 4:26); and if we love the Lord, we must hate sin (Ps. 97:10). But man's anger does not produce God's righteousness (1:20). In fact, anger is just the opposite of the patience God wants to produce in our lives as we mature in Christ (James 1:3-4).

I once saw a poster that read, "Temper is such a valuable thing, it is a shame to lose it!" It is temper that helps to give steel its strength. The person who cannot get angry at sin does not have much strength to fight it. James warns us against getting angry at God's Word because it reveals our sins to us. Like the man who broke the mirror because he disliked the image in it, people rebel against God's Word because it tells the truth about them and their sinfulness.

A prepared heart (1:21). James saw the human heart as a garden; if left to itself, the soil would produce only weeds. He urged us to "pull out the weeds" and prepare the soil for the "implanted Word of God." The phrase "superfluity of naughtiness" gives the picture of a garden overgrown with weeds that cannot be controlled. It is foolish to try to receive God's Word into an unprepared heart.

How do we prepare the soil of our hearts for God's Word? First, by confessing our sins and asking the Father to forgive us (1 John 1:9). Then, by meditating on God's love and grace and asking Him to "plow up" any hardness in our hearts, "Break up your fallow ground, and sow not among thorns" (Jer. 4:3). Finally, we must have an attitude of "meekness" (1:21). Meekness is the opposite of "wrath" in verses 19 and 20. When you receive the Word with meekness, you accept it, do not argue with it, and honor it as the Word of God. You do not try to twist it to conform it to your thinking.

If we do not receive the implanted Word, then we are deceiving ourselves. Christians who like to argue various "points of view" may be only fooling themselves. They think that their "discussions" are promoting spiritual growth, when in reality they may only be cultivating the weeds.

Practice the Word (1:22-25)

It is not enough to hear the Word; we must do it.
Many people have the mistaken idea that hearing
a good sermon or Bible study is what makes them
grow and get God's blessing. It is not the hearing
but *the doing* that brings the blessing. Too many
Christians mark their Bibles, but their Bibles never
mark them! If you think you are spiritual because
you hear the Word, then you are only kidding
yourself.

In the previous paragraph, James compared the
Word to seed; but in this paragraph, he compared
it to a mirror. There are two other references in
the Bible to God's Word as a mirror; and when you
put all three together, you discover three ministries
of the Word of God as a mirror.

Examination (1:23-25). This is the main purpose
for owning a mirror, to be able to see yourself and
make yourself look as clean and neat as possible.
As we look into the mirror of God's Word, we see
ourselves as we really are. James mentions several
mistakes people make as they look into God's
mirror.

First, *they merely glance at themselves.* They
do not carefully study themselves as they read the
Word. Many sincere believers read a chapter of
the Bible each day, but it is only a religious
exercise and they fail to profit from it personally.
Their conscience would bother them if they did
not have their daily reading, when actually their
conscience should bother them *because they read
the Word carelessly.* A cursory reading of the Bible
will never reveal our deepest needs. It is the difference between a candid photo and an X-ray.

The second mistake is that *they forget what they
see.* If they were looking deeply enough into their

hearts, what they would see would be unforgettable! We tend to smile at the "extremes" of people back in the days of the great revivals, but perhaps we could use some of that conviction. John Wesley wrote about a preaching service: "One before me dropped as dead, and presently a second, and a third. Five others sunk down in half an hour, most of whom were in violent agonies." (*Wesley's Journal* for June 22, 1739) Before we consign these people to some psychological limbo, remember how saints in the Bible responded to the true knowledge of their own hearts. Isaiah cried, "Woe is me! for I am undone!" (Isa. 6:5), and Peter cried, "Depart from me, for I am a sinful man, O Lord!" (Luke 5:8) Job was the most righteous man on earth in his day, yet he confessed, "I abhor myself, and repent in dust and ashes" (Job 42:6).

Mistake number three is: *they fail to obey what the Word tells them to do*. They think that *hearing* is the same as *doing*, and it is not. We Christians enjoy substituting *reading* for *doing*, or even *talking* for *doing*. We hold endless committee meetings and conferences about topics like evangelism and church growth, and think we have made progress. While there is certainly nothing wrong with conferences and committee meetings, they are sinful if they are a substitute for service.

If we are to use God's mirror profitably, then we must gaze into it carefully and with serious intent (1:25). No quick glances will do. We must examine our own hearts and lives in the light of God's Word. This requires time, attention, and sincere devotion. Five minutes with God each day will never accomplish a deep spiritual examination.

I have been fortunate with the doctors who have cared for me through the years, and I owe a great

deal to them. Each of them has possessed two
qualities that I have appreciated: they have spent
time with me and have not been in a hurry, and
they have always told me the truth. When Jesus,
the Great Physician (Matt. 9:12), examines us, He
uses His Word; and He wants us to give Him
sufficient time to do the job well. Perhaps one
reason we glance into the Word instead of gaze
into the Word is that we are afraid of what we
might see.

After seeing ourselves, we must remember what
we are and what God says, and we must *do the
Word.* The blessing comes in the doing, not in the
reading of the Word. "This man shall be blessed in
his doing" (1:25, literal translation). The emphasis
in James is on the practice of the Word. We are to
continue after reading the Word (1:25; see Acts
1:14, 2:42 and 46, 13:43, 14:22 and 26:22 for examples of this in the early church).

Why does James call the Word of God "the perfect law of liberty"? (v. 25) Because when we obey
it, God sets us free. "And I will walk at liberty:
for I seek Thy precepts" (Ps. 119:45). "Whosoever
committeth sin is the servant of sin (John 8:34).
"If ye continue in My Word, then are ye My
disciples indeed; and ye shall know the truth, and
the truth shall make you free" (John 8:31-32).

But *examination* is but the first ministry of the
mirror of the Word. There is a second ministry.

Restoration (Ex. 38:8). When he built the tabernacle, Moses took the metal looking glasses of the
women and from them made the laver. The laver
was a huge basin that stood between the brazen
altar of sacrifice and the holy place. (Read Ex.
30:17-21 for details.) The basin was filled with
water, and the priests washed their hands and feet

at the laver before they entered the holy place to minister.

Water for washing is a picture of the Word of God in its cleansing power. "Now ye are clean through the Word which I have spoken unto you" (John 15:3). The church is sanctified and cleansed "with the washing of water by the Word" (Eph. 5:26). When the sinner trusts Christ, he is once and for all washed clean (1 Cor. 6:9-11; Titus 3:4-6). But as the believer walks in this world, his hands and feet are defiled, and he needs cleansing (John 13:1-11).

The mirror of the Word not only examines us and reveals our sins, but it helps to cleanse us as well. It gives us the promise of cleansing (1 John 1:9) and, as we meditate on it, it cleanses the heart and the mind from spiritual defilement. It is the blood of Christ that cleanses the guilt, but the water of the Word helps to wash away the defilement.

Nathan's experience with David in 2 Samuel 12 helps to illustrate this truth. Nathan told David the story about the stolen ewe lamb, and David became angry at the sin described. "Thou art the man," said the prophet, and he held up the mirror of the Word for David to see himself. The result was confession and repentance: "I have sinned against the Lord!" The mirror of the Word did its work of examination.

But Nathan did not stop there. He also used the Word for *restoration*. "The Lord also hath put away thy sin; thou shalt not die" (2 Sam. 12:13). Here was the assurance of forgiveness and cleansing, and it came from the Word. David visited the laver and washed his hands and feet.

If we stop with examination and restoration, we

will miss the full benefit of the mirror ministry of
the Word. There is a third ministry.

Transformation (2 Cor. 3:18). After the Lord re-
stores us, He wants to change us so that we will
grow in grace and not commit that sin again. Too
many Christians confess their sins, and claim forgiveness, but never grow spiritually to conquer self
and sin.

Second Corinthians 3 is a discussion of the con-
trasts between the Old Covenant ministry of Law
and the New Covenant ministry of grace. The Law
is external, written on tables of stone; but salvation
means that God's Word is written on the heart.
The Old Covenant ministry condemned and killed;
but the New Covenant ministry brings forgiveness
and life. The glory of the Law gradually disap-
peared, but the glory of God's grace becomes
brighter and brighter. The Law was temporary,
but the New Covenant of grace is eternal.

Paul's illustration of this truth is Moses and his
veil. When Moses came down from the mount,
where he met God, his face was shining (Ex.
34:29-35). He did not want the Jews to see this
glory fading away, so he put a veil to hide it. When
he returned to the mount, he took off the veil. When
Jesus died, He rent the veil in the temple and
removed the veil between men and God. The Old
Testament prophet wore a veil to hide the fading
of the glory. The New Testament believer has an
unveiled face, and the glory gets greater and
greater!

You may explain 2 Corinthians 3:18 in this way:
"When the child of God looks into the Word of
God [the glass, the mirror], he sees the Son of God,
and he is transformed by the Spirit of God to share
in the glory of God!" The word *changed* in the

Greek gives us our English word "metamorphosis" —a change on the outside that comes from the inside. When an ugly worm turns into a beautiful butterfly, this is metamorphosis. When a believer spends time looking into the Word and seeing Christ, he is transformed: the glory on the inside is revealed on the outside.

It is this word that is translated "transfigured" in Matthew 17:2. The glory of Christ on the mount was not reflected; it was radiated from within. You will find the same word in Romans 12:2, "be ye transformed by the renewing of your mind." As we meditate on the Word, the Spirit renews the mind and reveals the glory of God. We do not become spiritual Christians overnight. It is a process, the work of the Spirit of God through the mirror of the Word of God.

The important thing is that we hide nothing. Take off the veil! "Search me, O God, and know my heart: try me, and know my thoughts: and see if there be any wicked way in me, and lead me in the way everlasting" (Ps. 139:23-24). "If we say that we have no sin, we deceive ourselves, and the truth is not in us" (1 John 1:8).

Our first responsibility is to receive the Word. Then, we must practice the Word; otherwise we are deceiving ourselves. This leads to a third responsibility.

Share the Word (1:26-27)

The word translated *religion* means "the outward practice, the service of a god." It is used only five times in the entire New Testament (James 1:26-27, Acts 26:5, and Col. 2:18, where it is translated "worshiping.") Pure religion has nothing to do with ceremonies, temples, or special days. Pure religion means practicing God's Word and sharing it with others, through speech, service, and separation from the world.

Speech (1:26). There are many references to speech in this letter, giving the impression that the tongue was a serious problem in the assembly. (See 1:19, 2:12, 3:1-3 and 14-18, 4:11-12.) It is the tongue that reveals the heart (Matt. 12:34-35); if the heart is right, the speech will be right. A controlled tongue means a controlled body (3:1ff).

Service (1:27a). After we have seen ourselves and Christ in the mirror of the Word, we must see others and their needs. Isaiah first saw the Lord, then himself, and then the people to whom he would minister (Isa. 6:1-8). Words are no substitute for deeds of love (James 2:14-18; 1 John 3:11-18). God does not want us to pay for others to minister as a substitute for our own personal service!

Separation from the world (1:27b). By "the world" James means "society without God." Satan is the prince of this world (John 14:30), and the lost are the children of this world (Luke 16:8). As the children of God, we are *in* the world physically but not *of* the world spiritually (John 17:11-16). We are sent *into* the world to win others to Christ (John 17:18). It is only as we maintain our separation from the world that we can serve others.

The world wants to "spot" the Christian and start to defile him. First, there is "friendship of the world" (James 4:4), which can lead to a love for the world (1 John 2:15-17). If we are not careful, we will become conformed to this world (Rom. 12:1-2), and the result is being condemned with the world (1 Cor. 11:32). This does not suggest that we lose our salvation, but that we lose all we have lived for. Lot is an illustration of this principle. First he pitched his tent toward Sodom, and then moved into Sodom. Before long, Sodom moved into him and he lost his testimony even with his own family. When judgment fell on Sodom, Lot lost everything. It was Abraham, the separated believer, the friend of God, who had a greater ministry to the people than did Lot, the friend of the world. It is not necessary for the Christian to get involved with the world to have a ministry to the world. Jesus was "unspotted" (1 Peter 1:19), and yet He was the friend of publicans and sinners. The best way to minister to the needs of the world is to be pure from the defilement of the world.

5

Rich Man, Poor Man

(JAMES 2:1–13)

Not only is the mature Christian patient in testing (James 1), but he also practices the truth. This is the theme of James 2. Immature people talk about their beliefs, but the mature person lives his faith. Hearing God's Word (James 1:22-25) and talking about God's Word can never substitute for doing God's Word.

Every believer has some statement of faith or personal expression of what he believes. Most churches have such statements and members are asked to subscribe to the statement and practice it. Most churches also have a "covenant" that they read publicly, often when they observe the Lord's Supper. Statements of faith and church covenants are good and useful, but they are not substitutes for doing God's will. As a pastor, I have heard believers read the church covenant and then come to a business meeting and act in ways completely contrary to the covenant.

James wanted to help us practice God's Word, so he gave us a simple test. He sent two visitors to a church service, a rich man and a poor man; and he watched to see how they were treated. *The way we behave toward people indicates what we really believe about God!* We cannot—and dare not—separate *human* relationships from *divine* fellowship. "If a man say, 'I love God,' and hateth his brother, he is a liar: for he that loveth not his brother whom he hath seen, how can he love God whom he hath not seen?" (1 John 4:20)

In this section, James examines four basic Christian doctrines in the light of the way we treat other people.

The Deity of Christ (2:1-4)

"My brothers, don't hold the faith of our Lord Jesus Christ, the Lord of Glory, by showing favoritism" (literal translation). Jewish people in that day coveted recognition and honor, and vied with one another for praise. Our Lord's parables in Luke 14:7-14 deal with the problem, and also His denunciation of the Pharisees in Matthew 23.

We have this same problem with us today. Pyramid climbers are among us, not only in politics, industry, and society, but also in the church. Almost every church has its cliques, and often, new Christians find it difficult to get in. Some church members use their offices to enhance their own images of importance. Many of the believers James wrote to were trying to seize spiritual offices, and James had to warn them (James 3:1).

Jesus did not respect persons. Even His enemies admitted, "You aren't swayed by men, because You pay no attention to who they are" (Matt. 22:16, NIV). Our Lord did not look at the outward

appearance; He looked at the heart. He was not
impressed with riches or social status. The poor
widow who gave her mite was greater in His eyes
than the rich Pharisee who boastfully gave his
large donation. Furthermore, He saw the potential
in the lives of sinners. In Simon, He saw a rock. In
Matthew, the publican, He saw a faithful disciple
who would one day write one of the four Gospels.
The disciples were amazed to see Jesus talking
with the sinful woman at the well of Sychar, but
Jesus saw in her an instrument for reaping a great
harvest.

We are prone to judge people by their past, not
their future. When Saul of Tarsus was converted,
the church in Jerusalem was afraid to receive him!
It took Barnabas, who believed in Saul's conversion,
to break down the walls (Acts 9:26-28). We are
also prone to judge by outward appearance rather
than by the inner attitude of the heart. We do not
enjoy sitting with certain people in church because
they "are not our kind of people." Jesus was the
Friend of sinners, though He disapproved of their
sins. It was not compromise, but compassion, that
caused Him to welcome them, and when they
trusted Him, forgive them.

Jesus was despised and rejected. This fact was
prophesied in Isaiah 53:1-3. He was "the poor man"
that was rejected by the self-righteous nation. Unlike the foxes and the birds, He had no home. He
grew up in the despised city of Nazareth in a home
that knew the feeling of poverty. Had you and I
met Him while He was ministering on earth, we
would have seen nothing physically or materially
that would attract us.

Yet, *He is the very glory of God!* In the Old
Testament, God's glory dwelled first in the taber-

nacle (Ex. 40:34-38), and then in the temple (1 Kings 8:10-11). When Jesus came to earth, God's glory resided in Him (John 1:14). Today, the glory of God dwells in the believer individually (1 Cor. 6:19-20), and the church collectively (Eph. 2:21-22).

The religious experts in Christ's day judged Him by their human standards, and they rejected Him. He came from the wrong city, Nazareth of Galilee. He was not a graduate of their accepted schools. He did not have the official approval of the people in power. He had no wealth. His followers were a nondescript mob and included publicans and sinners. *Yet He was the very glory of God!* No wonder Jesus warned the religious leaders, "Stop judging by mere appearances, and make a right judgment" (John 7:24, NIV).

Sad to say, we often make the same mistakes. When visitors come into our churches, we tend to judge them on what we see outwardly rather than what they are inwardly. Dress, color of skin, fashion, and other superficial things carry more weight than the fruit of the Spirit that may be manifest in their lives. We cater to the rich because we hope to get something out of them, and we avoid the poor because they embarrass us. Jesus did not do this, and He cannot approve of it.

How do we practice the deity of Christ in our human relationships? It is really quite simple: *look at everyone through the eyes of Christ.* If the visitor is a Christian, we can accept him because *Christ lives in him.* If he is not a Christian, we can receive him because *Christ died for him.* It is Christ who is the link between us and others, and He is a link of love. The basis for relationship with others is the Person and work of Jesus Christ. Any

other basis is not going to work. Furthermore,
God can use even the most unlikely person to
bring glory to His name. He used Peter and
Zaccheus and John Mark, and He can use that poor
man whom we might reject.

The Grace of God (2:5-7)

The emphasis here is on God's *choosing,* and this
involves the grace of God. If salvation were on
the basis of merit, it would not be by grace. Grace
implies God's sovereign choice of those who cannot earn and do not deserve His salvation (Eph.
1:4-7 and 2:8-10). God saves us completely on the
basis of the work of Christ on the cross and not
because of anything that we are or have.

God ignores *national* differences (Acts 10:34).
The Jewish believers were shocked when Peter
went to the Gentile household of Cornelius,
preached to the Gentiles, and even ate with them.
The topic of the first church council was, "Must a
Gentile become a Jew to become a Christian?"
(Acts 15) The answer the Holy Spirit gave them
was, "No!" In the sight of God, there is no difference
between Jew and Gentile when it comes to condemnation (Rom. 2:6-16) or salvation (Rom.
10:1-13.)

God also ignores *social* differences. Masters and
slaves (Eph. 6:9) and rich and poor are alike to
Him. James teaches us that the grace of God makes
the rich man poor, because he cannot depend on
his wealth; and it makes the poor man rich, because he inherits the riches of grace in Christ.
(Review James 1:9-11.) "The Lord Maketh poor,
and maketh rich: He bringeth low, and lifteth up.
He raiseth up the poor out of the dust, and lifteth
up the beggar from the dunghill, to set them among

princes, and to make them inherit the throne of glory" (1 Sam. 2:7-8a).

From the human point of view, God chooses the poor instead of the rich. "For ye see your calling, brethren, how that not many wise men after the flesh, not many mighty, not many noble, are called: but God hath chosen the foolish things of the world to confound the wise; and God hath chosen the weak things of the world to confound the things which are mighty" (1 Cor. 1:26-27). The poor of this world become rich in faith; as sons of God, they inherit the wealth of the kingdom.

It is possible to be poor in this world and rich in the next, or rich in this world and poor in the next (1 Tim. 6:17-18). Or, you could be poor both in this world and the next, or rich in this world and the next. It all depends on what you do with Christ and the material wealth He has given you. God promises the kingdom to "those that love Him" (James 2:5), not to those who love this world and its riches.

James gave a stern rebuke in verses 6 and 7. "When you despise the poor man, you are behaving like the unsaved rich people." In that day, it was easy for rich persons to exploit the poor, influence decisions at court, and make themselves richer. Unfortunately, we have the same sins being committed today; and these sins blaspheme the very name of Christ. Our Lord was poor, and He too was the victim of injustice perpetrated by the wealthy leaders of His day.

The doctrine of God's grace, if we really believe it, forces us to relate to people on the basis of God's plan and not on the basis of human merit or social status. A "class church" is not a church that magnifies the grace of God. When He died, Jesus

broke down the wall that separated Jews and
Gentiles (Eph. 2:11-22). But in His birth and life,
Jesus broke down the walls between rich and poor,
young and old, educated and uneducated. It is
wrong for us to build those walls again; we cannot
rebuild them if we believe in the grace of God.

The Word of God (2:8-11)

In recent years, believers have waged battles over
the inspiration and authority of the Word of God.
Certainly, it is a good thing to defend the truth of
God's Word, but we must never forget that *our
lives and ministries are the best defense.* D. L.
Moody often said, "Every Bible should be bound
in shoe leather!"

James reached back into the Old Testament for
one of God's laws, "Thou shalt love thy neighbor
as thyself" (Lev. 19:18). In His parable of the
Good Samaritan, Jesus told us that our neighbor is
anyone who needs our help (Luke 10:25-37). It
is not a matter of geography, but opportunity. The
important question is not, "Who is my neighbor?"
but "To whom can I be a neighbor?"

Why is "love thy neighbor" called "the royal
law"? For one thing, it was given by the King.
God the Father gave it in the Law, and God the
Son reaffirmed it to His disciples (John 13:34).
God the Spirit fills our hearts with God's love and
expects us to share it with others (Rom. 5:5). True
believers are "taught of God to love one another"
(1 Thes. 4:9).

But "love thy neighbor" is the royal law for a
second reason: *it rules all the other laws.* "Love is
the fulfilling of the law" (Rom. 13:10). There would
be no need for the thousands of complex laws if
each citizen truly loved his neighbors.

But the main reason why this is the royal law is that *obeying it makes you a king.* Hatred makes a person a slave, but love sets us free from selfishness and enables us to reign like kings. Love enables us to obey the Word of God and treat people as God commands us to do. We obey His Law, not out of fear, but out of love.

Showing respect of persons can lead a person into disobeying all of God's Law. Take any of the Ten Commandments and you will find ways of breaking it if you respect a person's social or financial status. Respect of persons could make you lie, for example. It could lead to idolatry (getting money out of the rich), or even mistreatment of one's parents. Once we start acting on the basis of respecting persons and rejecting God's Word, we are heading for trouble. And we need not break *all* of God's Law to be guilty. There is only one Lawgiver, and all of His Laws are from His mind and heart. If I disobey one law, I am capable of disobeying all of them; and by rebelling, I have already done so.

Christian love does not mean that I must *like* a person and agree with him on everything. I may not like his vocabulary or his habits, and I may not want him for an intimate friend. *Christian love means treating others the way God has treated me.* It is an act of the will, not an emotion that I try to manufacture. The motive is to glorify God. The means is the power of the Spirit within ("for the fruit of the Spirit is love"). As I act in love toward another, I may find myself drawn more and more to him, and I may see in him (through Christ) qualities that before were hidden to me.

Also, Christian love does not leave the person where it finds him. Love should help the poor man do better; love should help the rich man make better use of his God-given resources. Love always builds up (1 Cor. 8:1); hatred always tears down.

We only believe as much of the Bible as we practice. If we fail to obey the most important Word—"love thy neighbor as thyself"—then we will not do any good with the lesser matters of the Word. It was a glaring fault in the Pharisees that they were careful about the minor matters and careless about the fundamentals (Matt. 23:23). They broke the very Law they thought they were defending!

The Judgment of God (2:12-13)

Every orthodox statement of faith ends with a statement about the return of Jesus Christ and the final judgment. Not all Christians agree as to the details of these future events, but the certainty of them none denies. Nor would any deny the importance of a final judgment. Both Jesus (John 5:24) and Paul (Rom. 8:1) assured us that Christian believers will never be judged for their sins; but our works will be judged and rewarded (Rom. 14:10-13; 2 Cor. 5:9-10).

Our words will be judged. Note the words spoken to the two visitors in James 2:3. What we say to people, and how we say it, will come up before God. Even our careless words will be judged (Matt. 12:36). Of course, the words we speak come from the heart; so when God judges the words, He is examining the heart (Matt. 12:34-37). Jesus emphasized caution when speaking in some of His warnings in the Sermon on the Mount (Matt. 5:21-26, 33-37; 7:1-5, 21-23).

Our deeds will be judged. Read Colossians 3:22-

25 for additional insight. It is true that God remembers our sins against us no more (Jer. 31:34; Heb. 10:17); *but our sins affect our character and works.* We cannot sin lightly and serve faithfully. God forgives our sins when we confess them to Him, but He cannot change their consequences.

Our attitudes will be judged (2:13). James contrasted two attitudes: showing mercy to others, and refusing to show mercy. If we have been merciful toward others, God can be merciful toward us. However, we must not twist this truth into a lie. It does not mean that we *earn* mercy by showing mercy, because it is impossible to earn mercy. If it is earned, it is not mercy! Nor does it mean that we should "be soft on sin" and never judge it in the lives of others. "I don't condemn anybody," a man once told me, "and God won't condemn me." How wrong he was!

Mercy and justice both come from God, so they are not competitors. Where God finds repentance and faith, He is able to show mercy; where He finds rebellion and unbelief, He must administer justice. It is the heart of the sinner that determines the treatment he gets. Our Lord's parable in Matthew 18:21-35 illustrates the truth. The parable is not illustrating salvation, but forgiveness between fellow servants. If we forgive our brothers, then we have the kind of heart that is open toward the forgiveness of God.

We shall be judged "by the law of liberty." Why does James use this title for God's Law? For one thing, when we obey God's Law, it frees us from sin and enables us to walk in liberty (Ps. 119:45). Also, *law prepares us for liberty.* A child must be under rules and regulations because he is not mature enough to handle the decisions and demands of life. He is given *outward discipline* so that he might develop *inward discipline,* and one day be free of rules.

Liberty does not mean license. License (doing whatever I want to do) is the worst kind of bondage. Liberty means the freedom to be all that I can be in Jesus Christ. License is confinement; liberty is fulfillment.

Finally, the Word is called "the Law of liberty" because God sees our hearts and knows what we would have done had we been free to do so. The Christian student who obeys only because the school has rules is not really maturing. What will he do when he leaves the school? God's Word can change our hearts and give us the desires to do God's will, so that we obey from inward compulsion and not outward constraint.

There is one obvious message to this section: our beliefs should control our behavior. If we really believe that Jesus is the Son of God, and that God is gracious, His Word is true, and one day He will judge us, then our conduct will reveal our convictions. Before we attack those who do not have orthodox doctrine, we must be sure that we practice the doctrines we defend. Jonah had wonderful theology, but he hated people and was angry with God (Jonah 4).

One of the tests of the reality of our faith is how we treat other people. Can we pass the test?

6

False Faith

(JAMES 2:14–26)

Faith is a key doctrine in the Christian life. The sinner is saved by faith (Eph. 2:8-9), and the believer must walk by faith (2 Cor. 5:7). Without faith it is impossible to please God (Heb. 11:6); and whatever we do apart from faith is sin (Rom. 14:23).

Someone has said that faith is not "believing in spite of evidence, but obeying in spite of consequence." When you read Hebrews 11, you meet men and women who acted upon God's Word, no matter what price they had to pay. Faith is not some kind of nebulous feeling that we work up; faith is confidence that God's Word is true, and conviction that acting upon that Word will bring His blessing.

In this paragraph, James discussed the relationship between faith and works. This is an important discussion, for if we are wrong in this matter, we jeopardize our eternal salvation. What kind of

faith really saves a person? Is it necessary to perform good works in order to be saved? How can a
person tell whether or not he is exercising true
saving faith? James answers these questions by
explaining to us that there are three kinds of faith,
only one of which is true saving faith.

Dead Faith (2:14-17)

Even in the early church there were those who
claimed they had saving faith, yet did not possess
salvation. Wherever there is the true, you will find
the counterfeit. Jesus warned, "Not every one that
saith unto Me, 'Lord, Lord,' shall enter into the
kingdom of heaven; but he that doeth the will of
My Father which is in heaven" (Matt. 7:21).

People with dead faith substitute words for
deeds. They know the correct vocabulary for
prayer and testimony, and can even quote the
right verses from the Bible; but their walk does
not measure up to their talk. They think that their
words are as good as works, and they are wrong.

James gave a simple illustration. A poor believer
came into a fellowship, without proper clothing
and in need of food. The person with dead faith
noticed the visitor and saw his needs, but he did
not do anything to meet the needs. All he did was
say a few pious words! "Go, I wish you well; keep
warm and well fed" (2:16, NIV). But the visitor
went away just as hungry and naked as he came in!

Food and clothing are basic needs of every
human being, whether he is saved or unsaved.
"And having food and raiment let us be therewith
content" (1 Tim. 6:8). "Therefore take no thought,
saying, 'What shall we eat?' or, 'What shall we
drink?' or, 'Wherewithal shall we be clothed?' . . .
for your heavenly Father knoweth that ye have

need of all these things" (Matt. 6:31-32). Jacob included these basic needs in his prayer to God: "If God will be with me . . . and will give me bread to eat, and raiment to put on . . ." (Gen. 28:20).

As believers, we have an obligation to help meet the needs of people, no matter who they may be. "As we have therefore opportunity, let us do good unto all men, especially unto them who are of the household of faith" (Gal. 6:10). "Inasmuch as ye have done it unto one of the least of these My brethren, ye have done it unto Me" (Matt. 25:40).

To help a person in need is an expression of love, and faith works by love (Gal. 5:6). The Apostle John emphasized this aspect of good works. "If anyone has material possessions and sees his brother in need but has no pity on him, how can the love of God be in him? Dear children, let us not love with words or tongue but with actions and truth" (1 John 3:17-18, NIV). The priest and Levite in the parable of the Good Samaritan each had religious training, but neither of them paused to assist the dying man at the side of the road (Luke 10:25-37). Each of them would *defend* his faith, yet neither *demonstrated* that faith in loving works.

The question in verse 14 should read, "Can *that kind of faith* save him?" What kind? The kind of faith that is never seen in practical works. The answer is No! Any declaration of faith that does not result in a changed life and good works is a false declaration. That kind of faith is dead faith. "Even so faith, if it hath not works, is dead, being alone" (2:17). The great theologian, John Calvin, wrote, "It is faith alone that justifies, but faith that justifies can never be alone." The word *alone* in verse

17 simply means "by itself." True saving faith can
never be by itself: it always brings life, and life
produces good works.

The person with dead faith has only an intellectual experience. In his mind, he knows the
doctrines of salvation, but he has never submitted
himself to God and trusted Christ for salvation.
He knows the right words, but he does not back
up his words with his works. Faith in Christ brings
life (John 3:16), and where there is life there must
be growth and fruit. Three times in this paragraph,
James warns us that "faith without works is dead"
(2:17, 20, 26).

Beware of a mere intellectual faith. No man can
come to Christ by faith and remain the same any
more than he can come into contact with a 220-
volt wire and remain the same. "He that hath the
Son hath life; and he that hath not the Son of God
hath not life" (1 John 5:12). Dead faith is not saving
faith. Dead faith is counterfeit faith and lulls the
person into a false confidence of eternal life.

Demonic Faith (2:18-19)

James wanted to shock his complacent readers, so
he used demons as his illustration. In recent years
the church has rediscovered the reality and activity
of demons. When our Lord was ministering on
earth, He often cast out demons; and He gave that
power to His disciples. Paul often confronted
demonic forces in his ministry; and in Ephesians
6:10-20, he admonished the early Christians to
claim God's protection and defeat the spiritual
forces of wickedness.

It comes as shock to people that demons have
faith! What do they believe? For one thing, they
believe in the existence of God; they are neither

atheists nor agnostics. They also believe in the
deity of Christ. Whenever they met Christ when
He was on earth, they bore witness to His Sonship
(Mark 3:11-12). They believe in the existence of a
place of punishment (Luke 8:31); and they also
recognize Jesus Christ as the Judge (Mark 5:1-13).
They submit to the power of His Word.

"Hear, O Israel! The Lord our God is one Lord!"
(Deut. 6:4) This was the daily affirmation of faith
of the godly Jew. "You believe that there is one
God. Good! Even the demons believe that—and
shudder" (James 2:19, NIV). The man with dead
faith was touched only in his intellect; but the
demons are touched *also in their emotions*. They
believe and tremble.

But it is not a saving experience to believe and
tremble. A person can be enlightened in his mind
and even stirred in his heart and be lost forever.
True saving faith involves something more, something that can be seen and recognized: a changed
life. "Show me thy faith without thy works," challenged James, "and I will show thee my faith by
my works" (2:18).

How could a person show his faith without
works? Can a dead sinner perform good works?
Impossible! When you trust Christ, you are
"created in Christ Jesus unto good works, which
God hath before ordained that we should walk in
them" (Eph. 2:10). Being a Christian involves trusting Christ and living for Christ; you *receive* the
life, then you *reveal* the life. Faith that is barren
is not saving faith. The Greek word translated
"dead" in verse 20 carries the meaning of "barren
or idle," like money drawing no interest.

James has introduced us to two kinds of faith
that can never save the sinner: dead faith (the

intellect alone), and demonic faith (the intellect and the emotions). He closes this section by describing the only kind of faith that can save the sinner—dynamic faith.

Dynamic Faith (2:20-26)

Dynamic faith is faith that is real, faith that has power, faith that results in a changed life.

James *described* this true saving faith. To begin with, dynamic saving faith is *based on the Word of God.* We receive our spiritual rebirth through God's Word (James 1:18). We receive the Word and this saves us (1:21). "So then faith cometh by hearing, and hearing by the Word of God" (Rom. 10:17). James used Abraham and Rahab as illustrations of dynamic saving faith, since both of them heard and received the message of God through His Word.

Faith is only as good as its object. The man in the jungle bows before an idol of stone and trusts it to help him, but he receives no help. No matter how much faith a person may generate, if it is not directed at the right object, it will accomplish nothing. "I believe" may be the testimony of many sincere people, but the big question is, "In whom do you believe? What do you believe?" We are not saved by *faith in faith;* we are saved by faith in Christ as revealed in His Word.

Dynamic faith is based on God's Word, and *it involves the whole man.* Dead faith touches only the intellect; demonic faith involves both the mind and the emotions; but dynamic faith involves the will. The whole person plays a part in true saving faith. The mind understands the truth; the heart desires the truth; and the will acts upon the truth. The men and women of faith named in Hebrews 11 were people of action: God spoke and they obeyed. Again, "Faith is not believing in spite of evidence; faith is obeying in spite of consequence."

True saving faith *leads to action*. Dynamic faith is not intellectual contemplation or emotional consternation; it leads to obedience on the part of the will. And this obedience is not an isolated event: it continues throughout the whole life. It leads to works.

Many different kinds of works are named in the New Testament. "The works of the Law" (Gal. 2:16) relate to the sinner's attempt to please God by obeying the Law of Moses. Of course, it is impossible for a sinner to be saved through the works of the Law. "The works of the flesh" (Gal. 5:19) are done by unsaved people who live for the things of the old nature. There are also "wicked works" (Col. 1:21) and "dead works" (Heb. 9:14). Where there is dynamic faith—saving faith—you will always find good works.

James then *illustrated* his doctrine in the lives of two well-known Bible persons: Abraham and Rahab. You could not find two more different persons! Abraham was a Jew; Rahab was a Gentile. Abraham was a godly man, but Rahab was a sinful woman, a harlot. Abraham was the friend of God, while Rahab belonged to the enemies of God. What did they have in common? Both exercised saving faith in God.

You will want to read Genesis 15 and 22 to get the background facts for this illustration. God called Abraham out of Ur of the Chaldees to lead him into Canaan and to make out of him the great nation of Israel. It was through Israel that God would bring the Saviour into the world. Abraham's salvation experience is recorded in Genesis 15. At night, God showed His servant the stars and gave him a promise, "So shall thy seed [descendants] be!" How did Abraham respond? "And he believed in the Lord, and He [the Lord] counted it to him for righteousness" (Gen. 15:5-6).

The word *counted* is a legal or financial term; it means "to put to one's account." As a sinner, Abraham's spiritual bankbook was empty. He was bankrupt! But he trusted God, and God put *righteous* on Abraham's account. Abraham did not work for this righteousness; he received it as a gift from God. He was declared righteous by faith. He was justified by faith. (Read Rom. 4.)

Justification is an important doctrine in the Bible. Justification is the act of God whereby He declares the believing sinner righteous on the basis of Christ's finished work on the cross. It is not a process; it is an act. It is not something the sinner does; it is something God does for the sinner when he trusts Christ. It is a once-for-all event. It never changes.

How can you tell if a person is justified by faith if this transaction takes place between the sinner and God privately? Abraham's example answers that important question: the justified person has a changed life and obeys God's will. His faith is demonstrated by his works.

James used another event in Abraham's life, an event that took place many years after Abraham's conversion. This event is the offering up of Isaac on the altar (Gen. 22). Abraham was not saved by obeying God's difficult command. His obedience proved that he already was saved. "You see that his faith and his actions were working together, and his faith was made complete by what he did" (2:22, NIV). There is a perfect relationship between faith and works. As someone has expressed it, "Abraham was not saved by faith plus works, but by a faith that works."

How was Abraham "justified by works" (2:21) when he had already been "justified by faith"? (See Rom. 4.) By faith, he was justified *before God* and his righteousness declared; by works he was justified *before men* and his righteousness demonstrated. It is true that no humans actually saw Abraham put his son on the altar, but the inspired record in Genesis 22 enables us to see the event and witness Abraham's faith demonstrated by his works.

D. L. Moody often said, "Every Bible should be bound in shoe leather." He did not say that because he had been a successful shoe salesman; he said it because he was a dedicated Christian. Dynamic faith obeys God and proves itself in daily life and works. Alas, we still have church members today who fit the description given in Titus, "They profess that they know God, but in works they deny Him" (1:16). Paul also writes, "This is a faithful saying, and these things I will that thou affirm constantly, that they which have believed in God might be careful to maintain good works" (Titus 3:8).

His second illustration is Rahab, and the background for her is found in Joshua 2 and 6. Israel was about to invade their Promised Land and take the city of Jericho. Joshua sent spies into the city to get the lay of the land. There they met Rahab, a harlot, who protected them and affirmed that she believed in what God had said and what God was going to do. When the men departed, they promised to save her and her family when the city was taken; and this they did.

It is an exciting story. But in it is one of the Bible's great examples of saving faith (see Heb. 11:31). Rahab heard the Word and knew that her city was condemned. This truth affected her and her fellow citizens so that their hearts melted within them (Josh. 2:11). Rahab responded with her mind and her emotions; but she also responded with her will: *she did something about it*. She risked her own life to protect the Jewish spies, and she further risked her life by sharing the good news of deliverance with the members of her family. The Hebrew word translated "harlot" in Joshua 2 can also have the wider meaning of "an innkeeper." Rahab ran a guest house, so it was normal for the spies to go there. The Greek word "harlot" in James 2:25 definitely means an immoral person. This is also the meaning in Hebrews 11:31. Matthew 1:5 indicates she married into Israel and became an ancestress of our Lord. What grace! Rahab is one of the first soul-winners in the Bible, and you cannot help but compare her with the "bad Samaritan" in John 4.

Rahab could have had *dead* faith, a mere intellectual experience. Or she could have had *demonic* faith, her mind enlightened and her emotions stirred. But she exercised *dynamic* faith: her mind knew the truth, her heart was stirred by the truth, and her will acted upon the truth. She proved her faith by her works.

When you realize the small amount of information Rahab had, you can see how truly marvelous her faith really was. Today we have the full revelation of God through His Word and His Son. We live on the other side of Calvary, and we have the Holy Spirit to convict and to teach us the Word. "For unto whomsoever much is given, of him shall

be much required" (Luke 12:48). Her faith is an
indictment against the unbelief of sinners today.

James chapter 2 emphasized that the mature
Christian practices the truth. He does not merely
hold to ancient doctrines; he practices those doctrines in his everyday life. His faith is not the dead
faith of the intellectuals, or the demonic faith of
the fallen spirits. It is the dynamic faith of men
like Abraham and women like Rahab, faith that
changes a life and goes to work for God.

It is important that each professing Christian
examine his own heart and life and make sure that
he possesses true saving faith, dynamic faith. "Examine yourselves, whether ye be in the faith; prove
your own selves" (2 Cor. 13:5a). Satan is the great
deceiver; one of his devices is imitation. If he can
convince a person that counterfeit faith is true
faith, he has that person in his power.

Here are some questions we can ask ourselves
as we examine our hearts:

1. Was there a time when I honestly realized I
was a sinner and admitted this to myself and to
God?

2. Was there a time when my heart stirred me
to flee from the wrath to come? Have I ever seri-
ously been exercised over my sins?

3. Do I truly understand the Gospel, that Christ
died for my sins and arose again? Do I understand
and confess that I cannot save myself?

4. Did I sincerely repent of my sins and turn
from them? Or do I secretly love sin and want to
enjoy it? Or do I hate sin and fear God?

5. Have I trusted Christ and Christ alone for
my salvation? Do I enjoy a living relationship with
Him through the Word and in the Spirit?

6. Has there been a change in my life? Do I

maintain good works, or are my works occasional and weak? Do I seek to grow in the things of the Lord? Can others tell that I have been with Jesus?

7. Do I have a desire to share Christ with others? Or am I ashamed of Him?

8. Do I enjoy the fellowship of God's people? Is worship a delight to me?

9. Am I ready for the Lord's return? Or will I be ashamed when He comes for me?

To be sure, not every Christian has the same personal experience; and there are degrees of sanctification. But for the most part, this above spiritual inventory can assist a person in determining his true standing before God.

"Search me, O Lord, and know my heart: try me, and know my thoughts: and see if there be any wicked way in me, and lead me in the way everlasting" (Ps. 139:23-24).

7

The World's Smallest but Largest Troublemaker

(JAMES 3:1–12)

James has explained to us two characteristics of the mature Christian: he is patient in trouble (chap. 1) and he practices the truth (chap. 2). In this section, he shares the third characteristic of the mature believer: he has power over his tongue.

A pastor friend told me about a member of his church who was a notorious gossip. She would "hang on the phone" most of the day, sharing tidbits with any and all who would listen.

She came to the pastor one day and said, "Pastor, the Lord has convicted me of my sin of gossip. My tongue is getting me and others into trouble."

My friend knew she was not sincere because she had gone through that routine before. Guardedly he asked, "Well, what do you plan to do?"

"I want to put my tongue on the altar," she replied with pious fervor.

Calmly my friend replied, "There isn't an altar big enough," and he left her to think it over.

The Christians that James wrote to were apparently having serious problems with their tongues. James had warned them to be "swift to hear, slow to speak, slow to wrath" (James 1:19). The believer who does not bridle his tongue is not truly religious (1:26). We must speak and act as though we were already facing Christ in judgment (2:12). When you read passages like James 4:1 and 4:11-12, you get the impression that this assembly must have had some interesting meetings!

The power of speech is one of the greatest powers God has given us. With the tongue, man can praise God, pray, preach the Word, and lead the lost to Christ. What a privilege! But with that same tongue he can tell lies that could ruin a man's reputation or break a person's heart. The ability to speak words is the ability to influence others and accomplish tremendous tasks; and yet we take this ability for granted.

In order to impress upon us the importance of controlled speech, and the great consequences of our words, James gave us six pictures of the tongue: the bit, the rudder, fire, a poisonous animal, a fountain, and a fig tree. You can put these six pictures into three meaningful classifications that reveal the three powers of the tongue.

Power to Direct: the Bit and Rudder (3:1-4)

Apparently, everybody in the assembly wanted to teach and be a spiritual leader, for James had to warn them: "Not many of you should act as teachers, my brothers" (3:1, NIV). Perhaps they were impressed with the authority and prestige of the office, and forgot about the tremendous responsibility *and accountability*. Those who teach the Word face the stricter judgment. Teachers must use their tongue to share God's truth, and it is easy to commit sins of the tongue. Furthermore, teachers must practice what they teach; otherwise, their teaching is hypocrisy. Think of the damage that can be done by a teacher who is unprepared, or whose spiritual life is not up to par.

But teachers are not the only ones who are tempted and sin; every Christian must admit that "we all stumble in many ways" (3:2a, NIV). And sins of the tongue seem to head the list. The person who is able to discipline his tongue gives evidence that he can control his whole body. He proves that he is a mature (perfect) man.

Is James making a mistake by connecting sins of the tongue with sins committed by "the whole body"? No, because *words* usually lead to *deeds*. During World War II we were accustomed to seeing posters that read LOOSE LIPS SINK SHIPS! But loose lips also wreck lives. A person makes an unguarded statement and suddenly finds himself involved in a fight. His tongue has forced the rest of his body to defend itself.

In selecting the bit and the rudder ("helm" in verse 4 means "rudder"), James presented two items that are small of themselves, yet exercise great power, just like the tongue. A small bit enables the rider to control the great horse, and a small rudder enables the pilot to steer the huge ship. The tongue is a small member in the body, and yet it has the power to accomplish great things.

Both the bit and the rudder must overcome contrary forces. The bit must overcome the wild nature of the horse, and the rudder must fight the winds and currents that would drive the ship off its course. The human tongue also must overcome contrary forces. We have an old nature that wants to control us and make us sin. There are circumstances around us that would make us say things we ought not to say. Sin on the inside and pressures on the outside are seeking to get control of the tongue.

This means that both the bit and the rudder must be under the control of a strong hand. The expert horseman keeps the mighty power of his steed under control, and the experienced pilot courageously steers the ship through the storm. When Jesus Christ controls the tongue, then we need not fear saying the wrong things—or even saying the right things in a wrong way! "Death and life are in the power of the tongue," warned Solomon (Prov. 18:21). No wonder David prayed, "Set a watch, O Lord, before my mouth; keep the door of my lips. Incline not my heart to any evil thing" (Ps. 141:3-4a). David knew that *the heart* is the key to right speech. "Out of the abundance of the heart the mouth speaketh" (Matt. 12:34b). When Jesus Christ is the Lord of the heart, then He is Lord of the lips too.

The bit and rudder have the power to direct, which means *they affect the lives of others*. A runaway horse or a shipwreck could mean injury or death to pedestrians or passengers. The words we speak affect the lives of others. A judge says "Guilty!" or "Not Guilty!" and those words affect the destiny of the prisoner, his family, and his friends. The President of the United States speaks a few words and signs some papers and the nation is at war. Even a simple "Yes" or "No" from the lips of a parent can greatly affect the direction of a child's life.

Never underestimate the guidance you give by the words you speak or do not speak. Jesus spoke to a woman at a well, and her life and the life of her neighbors experienced a miraculous change (John 4). Peter preached at Pentecost and 3,000 souls came to salvation through faith in Christ (Acts 2).

On April 21, 1855, Edward Kimball went into a Boston shoestore and led young Dwight L. Moody to Christ. The result: one of history's greatest evangelists, a man whose ministry still continues. The tongue has the power to direct others to the right choices.

It would do us all good to read frequently the Book of Proverbs, and to note especially the many references to speech. "A soft answer turneth away wrath: but grievous words stir up anger" (Prov. 15:1). "Lying lips are an abomination to the Lord" (Prov. 12:22). "In the multitude of words there wanteth not sin: but he that refraineth his lips is wise" (Prov. 10:19). Yes, the tongue is like a bit and a rudder: it has the power to direct. How important it is that our tongues direct people in the right way!

Power to Destroy: the Fire and Animal (3:5-8)

I was visiting the used bookstores along Charing Cross Road in London, and I remarked to a clerk that there were not as many stores as I expected. "There's a reason for that," he replied. "One night during World War II, the incendiary bombs hit and the fires destroyed at least a million books!"

On another occasion, a friend was taking my wife and me on a tour of the beautiful forests in California, and we came to an ugly section that was burned out. Not only was the face of nature scarred, but millions of dollars of valuable timber had been wiped out. "Somebody's lit cigarette," my friend commented as we drove past the blackened earth.

A fire can begin with just a small spark, but it can grow to destroy a city. A fire reportedly started in the O'Leary barn in Chicago at 8:30 P.M., October 8, 1871; and because that fire spread, over 100,000 people were left homeless, 17,500 buildings were destroyed, and 300 people died. It cost the city over $400,000,000.

Our words can start fires. "Where no wood is, there the fire goeth out: so where there is no talebearer, the strife ceaseth. As coals are to burning coals, and wood to fire; so is a contentious man to kindle strife (Prov. 26:20-21). In some churches, there are members or officers who cannot control their tongues, and the result is destruction. Let them move out of town or be replaced in office, and a beautiful spirit of harmony and love takes over.

Like a fire, the tongue can "heat things up." David wrote: "I said, 'I will take heed to my ways, that I sin not with my tongue'. . . . My heart was not within me, while I was musing the fire burned; then spake I with my tongue" (Ps. 39:1a, 3). Have you ever had that experience? Of course you have! A hot head and a hot heart can lead to burning words that later we will regret. David had a temper, and he had to have God's help in controlling it. No wonder Solomon wrote, "He who restrains his word has knowledge, and he who has a cool spirit is a man of understanding" (Prov. 17:27, NASB). "He who is slow to anger has great understanding, but he who is quick-tempered exalts folly" (Prov. 14:29. NASB).

Fire not only starts small and grows, and creates heat; it also defiles. A friend of mine suffered a fire in the basement of his house, and the smoke and fire damage so soiled the upstairs of the house that the family had to move out while the house was redecorated. Fiery words can defile a home, a Sunday School class, a church. The only thing that can wash away that defilement is the blood of Jesus Christ.

Fire burns and hurts, and our words can burn and hurt. One of the sorrows our Lord had to bear when He was here on earth was the way His enemies talked about Him. They called Him a "man gluttonous and a winebibber" (Matt. 11:19) because He graciously accepted invitations to dine with people the Pharisees did not like. When He performed miracles, they said He was in league with Satan. Even when He was dying on the cross, His enemies could not let Him alone but threw vicious taunts into His face.

Fire spreads, and the more fuel you give it, the faster and farther it will spread. The tongue "setteth on fire the course of nature" (James 3:6), or "sets the whole course of his life on fire" (NIV). James suggests that all of life is connected like a wheel, and therefore we cannot keep things from spreading. A person's entire life can be injured or destroyed by the tongue. Time does not correct the sins of the tongue. We may confess our sins of speech, but the fire keeps on spreading.

As it spreads, fire destroys; and the words we speak have the power to destroy. For every word in Hitler's book, *Mein Kampf*, 125 lives were lost in World War II. Our own words may not have caused wars or wrecked cities, but they can break hearts and ruin reputations. They can also destroy souls by sending them into eternity without Christ. How important it is for us to let our speech "be

always full of grace, seasoned with salt" (Col. 4:6,
NIV).

Not only is the tongue like a fire, but it is also
like a dangerous animal. It is restless and cannot
be ruled (unruly), and it seeks its prey and then
pounces and kills. My wife and I once drove
through a safari park, admiring the animals as
they moved about in their natural habitat. But
there were warning signs posted all over the park:
DO NOT LEAVE YOUR CAR! DO NOT OPEN
YOUR WINDOWS! Those "peaceful animals" were
capable of doing great damage, and even killing.

Some animals are poisonous, and some tongues
spread poison. The deceptive thing about poison
is that it works secretly and slowly, and then kills.
How many times has some malicious person in-
jected a bit of poison into the conversation, hoping
it would spread and finally get to the person he or
she wanted to hurt? As a pastor, I have seen
poisonous tongues do great damage to individuals,
families, classes, and entire churches. Would you
turn hungry lions or angry snakes loose in your
Sunday morning service? Of course not! But unruly
tongues accomplish the same results.

James reminds us that animals can be tamed;
and, for that matter, fire can be tamed. When you
tame an animal, you get a worker instead of a
destroyer. When you control fire, you generate
power. The tongue cannot be tamed by man, but it
can be tamed by God. Your tongue need not be
"set on fire of hell" (3:6). Like the Apostles at
Pentecost, it can be set on fire from heaven! If
God lights the fire and controls it, then the tongue
can be a mighty tool for the winning of the lost
and the building up of the church. The important
thing, of course, is the heart; for it is "out of the

abundance of the heart that the mouth speaketh" (Matt. 12:34). If the heart is filled with hatred, Satan will light the fire. But if the heart is filled with love, God will light the fire.

Power to Delight: the Fountain and Tree (3:9-12)

The fountain, of course, provides the cool water that man needs to stay alive. In Oriental countries, the presence of a freshwater fountain is a great blessing to a village. Man needs water not only for drinking, but also for washing, cooking, farming, and a host of other activities so necessary to life.

"The words of a man's mouth are as deep waters, and the wellspring of wisdom as a flowing brook" (Prov. 18:4). "The mouth of a righteous man is a well of life" (Prov. 10:11). "The law of the wise is a fountain of life, to depart from the snares of death" (Prov. 13:14). These verses parallel what James has written and underscore the importance of our words.

Water is life-giving, and our words can give life. However, if water is not controlled, it brings death and destruction. The famous Johnstown, Pennsylvania flood of 1889 took 2,200 lives and destroyed $10 million in property. "Death and life are in the power of the tongue" (Prov. 18:21).

However, when we bend over a fountain for a drink of cool water, we rarely think of floods. We think only of the precious gift of refreshment that comes with a drink of water. We could not be healthy without water. "There is that speaketh like the piercings of a sword: but the tongue of the wise is health" (Prov. 12:18). Paul's prayer was that he might "refresh" the saints in Rome when he came to them (Rom. 15:32). He often named

Christians who had refreshed him (1 Cor. 16:18; Phile. 7, 20).

Water also cleanses. There was a laver in the Old Testament tabernacle and temple, provided for the cleansing of the priests' hands and feet. God's Word is the spiritual water that cleanses us (John 15:3; Eph. 5:26-27). But our words to others can also help to cleanse and sanctify them. Our words ought to be like that river described in Ezekiel 47 that brought life to everything it touched.

The tongue is also delightful because it is like a tree. In Bible lands, trees are vitally important to the economy: they help to hold down the soil; they provide beauty and shade; and they bear fruit. Our words can help to shelter and encourage a weary traveller, and can help to feed a hungry soul. "The lips of the righteous feed many" (Prov. 10:21). Jesus said, "The words that I speak unto you, they are spirit, and they are life" (John 6:63b). As we share His Word with others, we feed them and encourage them along the way.

The most important thing about a tree is the root system. If the roots do not go down deep, the tree will not grow in a healthy manner. If we are rooted in the things of the Lord, then our words will be the fruit of our fellowship with Him. We will be like that "blessed man" in Psalm 1 and produce fruit in due season. One reason our Lord was able to say the right words at the right times was because He communed with His Father and heard from heaven each day. Listen to His testimony:

"The Lord hath given Me the tongue of the learned, that I should know how to speak a word in season to him that is weary: He wakeneth morning by morning, He wakeneth Mine ear to hear as the learned" (Isa. 50:4). "And in the morning, rising up a great while before day, He went out, and departed into a solitary place, and there prayed" (Mark 1:35).

If you and I are going to have tongues that delight, then we must meet with the Lord each day and learn from Him. We must get our "spiritual roots" deep into His Word. We must pray and meditate and permit the Spirit of God to fill our hearts with God's love and truth.

But James issued a warning: a fountain cannot give forth two kinds of water, and a tree cannot bear two different kinds of fruit. We expect the fountain to flow with sweet water at all times, and we expect the fig tree to bear figs and the olive tree to bear olives. Nature reproduces after its kind.

If the tongue is inconsistent, there is something radically wrong with the heart. I heard about a professing Christian who got angry on the job and let loose with some oaths. Embarrassed, he turned to his partner and said, "I don't know why I said that. It really isn't in me." His partner wisely replied, "It had to be in you or it couldn't have come out of you." When Peter was out of fellowship with Christ, he uttered some oaths; but he went out and wept bitterly and confessed his sins.

The tongue that blesses the Father, and then turns around and curses men made in God's image, is in desperate need of spiritual medicine! How easy it is to sing the hymns during the worship service, then after the service, get into the family car and argue and fight all the way home! "My brethren, these things ought not so to be."

The problem, of course, is not the tongue; it is

the heart. It is easy to have "bitter envying and strife" in our hearts (3:14). "But those things which proceed out of the mouth come forth from the heart; and they defile the man" (Matt. 15:18). "Keep thy heart with all diligence, for out of it are the issues of life" (Prov. 4:23). As we fill our hearts with God's Word, and yield to the Holy Spirit, He can use us to bring delight to others, and we will be refreshing fountains and trees.

As I close this chapter, let me suggest that you start using the "Twelve Words that can Transform Your Life." If you use these words *and sincerely mean what you say from your heart,* you will find that God will use you to be a blessing and encouragement to others. There are only twelve of them, but they work.

"Please" and *"Thank you"* When you use these three words, you are treating others like people and not things. You are showing appreciation.

"I'm sorry." These two words have a way of breaking down walls and building bridges.

"I love you." Too many people read "romance" into these words, but they go much deeper than that. As Christians, we should love the brethren and even love our enemies. "I love you" is a statement that can carry tremendous power.

"I'm praying for you." And be sure that you are. When you talk to God about people, then you can talk to people about God. Our private praying for people helps us in our public meeting with people. Of course, we never say "I'm praying for you" in a boastful way, as though we are more spiritual than others. We say it in an encouraging way, to let others know that we care enough for them to meet them at the throne of grace.

Yes, the smallest but largest troublemaker in all

the world is the tongue. But it does not have to be a troublemaker! God can use our tongues to direct others into the way of life, and to delight them in the trials of life. The tongue is a little member, but it has great power.

Give God your tongue and your heart each day and ask Him to use you to be a blessing to others.

8

Where to Obtain Wisdom

(JAMES 3:13–18)

Wisdom was an important thing to Jewish people. They realized that it was not enough to have knowledge; you had to have wisdom to be able to use that knowledge correctly. All of us know people who are very intelligent, perhaps almost geniuses, and yet who seemingly are unable to carry out the simplest tasks of life. They can run computers but they cannot manage their own lives! "Wisdom is the principal thing; therefore get wisdom" (Prov. 4:7).

James continued to exhort the people in the assembly who wanted to be teachers of the Word (James 3:1). It is not enough simply to stand before the people and say words; *you must have something to say.* This is where spiritual wisdom comes in. Knowledge enables us to take things apart, but wisdom enables us to put things together and relate God's truth to daily life. All of us have heard preachers and teachers who say many good things, but who somehow miss the heart of God's message and fail to relate truth to everyday life. It is this kind of "knowledge without wisdom" that James is writing about. He is contrasting true wisdom and false wisdom in three different aspects.

Contrast in Origins (3:15, 17a)

The true wisdom comes from above, but the false wisdom comes from below. In other words, there is a "heavenly wisdom" that comes from God, and there is a "man-made wisdom" that does not come from God. Whatever does not come from God is destined to fail, no matter how successful it may seem at the time.

The Bible contains many examples of the folly of man's wisdom. The building of the Tower of Babel seemed like a wise enterprise, but it ended in failure and confusion (Gen. 11:1-9). It seemed wise for Abraham to go to Egypt when famine came to Canaan, but the results proved otherwise (Gen. 12:10-20). King Saul thought it was wise to put his own armor on young David for the lad's battle with Goliath, but God's plan was otherwise (1 Sam. 17:38ff). The disciples thought it was wise to dismiss the great crowd and let them find their own food; but Jesus took a few loaves and fishes and fed the multitude. The Roman "experts" in Acts 27 thought it was wise to leave port and set sail for Rome, even though Paul disagreed; and the storm that followed proved that Paul's wisdom was better than their expert counsel. They lived to regret it, but they lived!

What is the origin of man's wisdom? "This wisdom descendeth not from above, but is earthly, sensual, devilish" (James 3:15). The believer has three enemies: the world, the flesh, and the devil

(Eph. 2:1-3). These enemies are suggested by the terms "earthly, sensual, devilish."

There is a "wisdom of this world" (1 Cor. 1:20-21). Do not confuse the world's *knowledge* and the world's *wisdom*. Certainly, there is a great deal of knowledge in this world, and we all benefit from it; but there is not much wisdom. Man unlocks the secrets of the universe, but he does not know what to do with them. Almost everything he discovers or devises turns against him. Over a century ago, Henry David Thoreau warned that we had "improved means to unimproved ends."

Whenever I ride a bus or elevated train in the city, I often think of the man in Boston who was entertaining a famous Chinese scholar. He met his Oriental friend at the train station and rushed him to the subway. As they ran through the subway station, the host panted to his guest, "If we run and catch this next train, we will save three minutes!" To which the patient Chinese philosopher replied, "And what significant thing shall we do with the three minutes we are saving?"

The world by its wisdom knew not God, and in its wisdom rejects the very Gospel of God. "For the preaching of the cross is to them that perish foolishness" (1 Cor. 1:18). Any person enamored with the wisdom of this world ought to read the first two chapters of 1 Corinthians and notice how much Paul has to say about God's wisdom and man's wisdom. Man's wisdom is foolishness to God (1 Cor. 1:20), and God's wisdom is foolishness to man (1 Cor. 2:14). Man's wisdom comes from reason, while God's wisdom comes from revelation. Man's worldly wisdom will come to nothing (1 Cor. 1:19), while God's wisdom will endure forever.

Because the world has turned from God, it has

lost its wisdom. Every increase in man's knowledge only magnifies the problems. "The fear of the Lord is the beginning of wisdom; and the knowledge of the holy is understanding" (Prov. 9:10). "There is no fear of God before their eyes" (Rom. 3:18).

But this false wisdom has another source: it is "sensual," that is, it is "natural." The Greek word is *psukikos*, which comes from the Greek word *psuke* meaning "life," or "soul." Our English word "psychology" is derived from it. In 1 Corinthians 2:14 and 15:44 and 46, *psukikos* is translated "natural," referring to the opposite of "spiritual." In Jude 19 it is translated "sensual." The main idea seems to be that of man's fallen nature as opposed to the new nature given by God. There is a wisdom that gets its origin in man's nature totally apart from the Spirit of God.

But this "wisdom that is from beneath" is also "devilish." Perhaps the best translation is *demonic*. Beginning with Genesis 3, where Satan successfully deceived Eve, and continuing through the entire Bible, there is a "wisdom of Satan" at work, fighting against the wisdom of God. Satan convinced Eve that she would be like God. He told her that the tree would make her wise. Ever since that event, people have continued to believe Satan's lies and have tried to become their own gods (Rom. 1:18-25). Satan is cunning; he is the old serpent! He has wisdom that will confound and confuse you if you do not know the wisdom of God.

In contrast to the wisdom that is earthly, sensual, and devilish, James describes a "wisdom that is from above" (3:17). "Every good gift and every perfect gift is from above" (James 1:17). The Christian looks up to heaven for all that he needs. His citizenship is in heaven (Phil. 3:20), just as his Father is in

heaven (Matt. 6:9). His treasures are in heaven, not
on earth (Matt. 6:19ff). He was born from above
(John 3:1-7) when he trusted Jesus Christ. The believer's home is in heaven (John 14:1-6) and his
hope is in heaven. He sets his affection and attention on things above, not on earthly things (Col.
3:1-4).

What is the Christian's wisdom? Does he look to
the philosophies of this world? No! To begin with,
Jesus Christ is our wisdom (1 Cor. 1:24, 30). In
Jesus Christ "are hid all the treasures of wisdom
and knowledge" (Col. 2:3). The first step toward
true wisdom is the receiving of Jesus Christ as
Saviour.

The Word of God is also our wisdom. "Behold, I
have taught you statutes and judgments. . . . Keep
therefore and do them; for this is your wisdom and
your understanding in the sight of the nations"
(Deut. 4:5a and 6a). The Scriptures are able to
make us "wise unto salvation" (2 Tim. 3:15).

James 1:5 indicates that we find wisdom through
believing prayer. "If any of you lack wisdom, let
him ask of God." The Holy Spirit of God is "the
Spirit of wisdom and revelation" (Eph. 1:17) and
He directs us in the wisest paths as we trust the
Word and pray.

The origin of true spiritual wisdom is God. To
get your wisdom from any other source is to ask for
trouble. There is no need to get the counterfeit
wisdom of the world, the wisdom that caters to the
flesh and accomplishes the work of the devil. Get
your wisdom from God!

Contrast in Operations (3:13-14, 17)
The wisdom from above, God's wisdom, operates in
a different way from the wisdom that is "earthly,

sensual, devilish." Since they originate from radically different sources, they must operate in opposite ways.

What are the evidences of false wisdom?

Envy (3:14). This word carries the meaning of selfish ambition and zeal. It ties in with the first verse of chapter 3, where James warned them not to be ambitious for spiritual offices. The wisdom of the world says, "Promote yourself. You're as good as the other candidates, maybe better! The wheel that squeaks the loudest gets the grease." Sad to say, there is a great deal of selfish, carnal promotion among God's people. Even the first Apostles argued over who was the greatest in the kingdom.

It is easy to go on an ego trip under the guise of spiritual zeal. The Pharisees used their religious activities to promote the praise of men (Matt. 6:1-18). We ought to be zealous in the things of the Lord, but we must be sure that our motives are right. The wisdom of this world exalts man and robs God of glory. In 1 Corinthians 1:17ff, Paul discussed the wisdom of God and the wisdom of this world, and he explained why God works as He does: "That no flesh should glory in His presence" (v. 29). He concluded the section with the admonition, "He that glorieth, let him glory in the Lord" (v. 31).

Is our zeal for the Lord spiritual or carnal? Do we rejoice when others succeed, or do we have secret envy and criticism? Do we feel burdened when others fail, or are we glad? When the wisdom of the world gets into the church, there is a great deal of fleshly promotion and human glorification. Beware!

Strife (3:14). This word means "party spirit." It was used by the Greeks to describe a politician out

canvassing for votes. The world's wisdom says,
"Get all the support you can! Ask the people in the
church if they are for you or against you!" Of course,
this spirit of self-seeking only creates rivalry and
division in the church. "Let nothing be done
through strife or vainglory; but in lowliness of
mind let each esteem other better than [more
important than] themselves" (Phil. 2:3).

Boasting (3:14). Pride loves to boast, and nothing
is prouder than the wisdom of men. There is a way
to report blessings so that God gets the glory, but
there is also an approach that gives the praise to
men. It is tragic to see mutual admiration societies
among God's people. In 2 Corinthians 10, when
Paul was forced to boast about his ministry, he was
careful to give the glory to God. "Of course, we
shouldn't dare include ourselves in the same class
as those who write their own testimonials, or even
to compare ourselves with them! All they are doing, of course, is to measure themselves by their
own standards or by comparisons within their own
circle, and that doesn't make for accurate estima-
tion, you may be sure" (2 Cor. 10:12, PH).

When God's wisdom is at work, there is a sense
of humility and submission, and you want God to
get all the glory. You have no desire to compare
yourself with any other Christian, because you see
only Christ—and compared with Him, all of us still
have a long way to go!

Deceit (3:14). "Lie not against the truth." The
sequence is not difficult to understand. First, there
is selfish ambition that leads to party spirit and
rivalry. In order to "win the election" we must re-
sort to boasting; *and boasting usually involves lies!*
A man's life is not read in his press releases; it is
read by the Lord in his heart. "Therefore judge

nothing before the time, until the Lord come, who both will bring to light the hidden things of darkness, and will make manifest the counsels of the hearts: and then shall every man have praise of God" (1 Cor. 4:5).

What a relief it is to turn to the evidences of true spiritual wisdom.

Meekness (3:13). Meekness is not weakness; it is power under control. The meek person does not selfishly assert himself. The Greek word was used for a horse that had been broken so that his power was under control. The meek person seeks only the glory of God and does not cater to the praises of men. Meekness is a fruit of the Spirit (Gal. 5:23); it cannot be manufactured by man. There is a false humility that some people mistake for meekness, but it is only counterfeit.

The phrase, "meekness of wisdom," is an interesting one (James 3:3). Meekness is the right use of power, and wisdom is the right use of knowledge. They go together. The truly wise person will show in his daily life ("conversation" means "behavior") that he is a child of God. Attitude and action go together.

Purity (3:17). "First pure" indicates the importance of holiness. God is holy; therefore the wisdom from above is pure. The idea behind this word is "chaste, free from defilement." James used it again in 4:8—"purify your hearts," or, "make chaste your hearts." God's wisdom leads to purity of life. Man's wisdom leads to sin. There is a spiritual purity that results in a chaste relationship with the Lord (2 Cor. 11:3); and there is a worldliness that makes the person a spiritual adulterer (James 4:4).

Peace (3:17). Man's wisdom leads to competition, rivalry, and war (James 4:1-2); but God's wisdom leads to peace. It is a peace based on holiness, not on compromise. God never has "peace at any price." The peace of the church is not more important than the purity of the church. If the church is pure, devoted to God, then there will be peace. "And the work of righteousness shall be peace, and the effect of righteousness quietness and assurance forever" (Isa. 32:17). The church can never have peace by sweeping sins under the rug and pretending they are not there. Man's wisdom says, "Cover up sin! Keep things together!" God's wisdom says, "Confess sin and My peace will keep things together!"

Gentleness (3:17). Matthew Arnold liked to call this "sweet reasonableness." It carries the meaning of moderation without compromise, gentleness without weakness. The gentle person does not deliberately cause fights, but neither does he compromise the truth in order to keep peace. Carl Sandburg described Abraham Lincoln as a man of "velvet steel." That is a good description of gentleness.

Compliance (3:17). God's wisdom makes the believer agreeable and easy to live with and work with. Man's wisdom makes a person hard and stubborn. The compliant person is willing to hear all sides of a question, but he does not compromise his own convictions. He can disagree without being disagreeable. He is "swift to hear, slow to speak, slow to wrath" (James 1:19). Many people think that stubbornness is conviction, and they must have their own way. When God's wisdom is at work, there is a willingness to listen, think, pray, and obey whatever God reveals. "Yielding to persuasion" is another translation of this word.

Mercy (3:17). To be "full" of something means

to be "controlled by." The person who follows God's wisdom is controlled by mercy. "Be ye therefore merciful, as your Father also is merciful" (Luke 6:36). God in His grace gives us what we do not deserve, and in His mercy He does not give us what we do deserve. Our Lord's parable of the Good Samaritan illustrates the meaning of mercy (Luke 10:25-37). For a Samaritan to care for a Jewish stranger was an act of mercy. He could gain nothing from it, except the blessing that comes from doing the will of God; and the victim could not pay him back. That is mercy.

Good fruits (3:17). People who are faithful are fruitful. God's wisdom does not make a life empty; it makes it full. The Spirit produces fruit to the glory of God (see John 15:1-16). The lawyer in Luke 10:25-37 was willing to *discuss* the subject of neighborliness, but he was unwilling to be a neighbor and help someone else. God's wisdom is practical; it changes the life and produces good works to the glory of God.

Decisiveness (3:17). The word suggests singleness of mind and is the opposite of "wavering" (James 1:6). When you lean on the world's wisdom, you are pressured from one side and then another to change your mind or take a new viewpoint. When you have God's wisdom, you need not waver; you can be decisive and not be afraid. Wisdom from above brings strength from above.

Sincerity (3:17). The Greek word translated *hypocrite* in our New Testament means "one who wears a mask, an actor." When man's wisdom is at work, there must be insincerity and pretense. When God's wisdom is at work, there is openness and honesty, "speaking the truth in love" (Eph. 4:15). Wherever you find God's people pretending and hiding, you can be sure the wisdom of this world is governing their ministry. "Religious politics" is an abomination to God. "Faith is living without scheming."

There is quite a contrast between the operation of God's wisdom and the operation of the wisdom of this world. It would be profitable for church officers and leaders to evaluate their own lives and their ministries in the light of what James has written. While the local church is an organization, it cannot depend on the "Madison Avenue" methods that make secular businesses succeed. God's ways and God's thoughts are far above us! "Now we have received, not the spirit of the world, but the Spirit which is of God; that we might know the things that are freely given to us of God" (1 Cor. 2:12).

Contrast in Outcomes (3:16, 18)

Origin determines outcome. Worldly wisdom will produce worldly results; spiritual wisdom will give spiritual results.

Worldly wisdom produces trouble (3:16). Envy, strife, confusion, evil works. It does not appear that God was at work in that assembly. In Chapter 4, James would deal with the "wars and fightings" among the believers. Wrong thinking produces wrong living. One reason the world is in such a mess is because men have refused to accept the wisdom of God.

The word translated *confusion* means "disorder that comes from instability." It is related to "unstable" in James 1:8 and "unruly" in James 3:8. Read 2 Corinthians 12:20 and you will get a description of a church that is confused. Jesus used this word to describe the convulsions of the world in the last days (Luke 21:9).

Jealousy, competition, party spirit—all of these contribute to confusion. The Tower of Babel in Genesis 11 is a good illustration of this fact. From man's point of view, the building of the tower was a wise thing; but from God's viewpoint, the project was stupid and sinful. The result? Confusion. Even today, we use the word "babel" to mean "confusion."

Confusion sets the stage for "every evil work" (James 3:16). *Evil* here means "worthless, of no account." It reminds us of the "wood, hay, stubble" of 1 Corinthians 3:12. A ministry operating in the wisdom of this world may appear to be great and successful, but in the day of judgment it may burn up. "Therefore judge nothing before the time" (1 Cor. 4:5). The church at Smyrna thought it was poor, but the Lord said it was rich; while the "rich church" at Laodicea was declared to be poor (Rev. 2:9 and 3:14-22).

The most important thing we can do in our local churches is measure our ministries by the Word of God, not by the wisdom of men. The many battles among Christians, the church splits, the absence of purity and peace, all suggest that something is wrong. Perhaps that "something" is the absence of the wisdom of God.

God's wisdom produces blessing (3:18). James returned to that word, *fruit.* There is a vast difference between man-made results and God-given fruit. Fruit is the product of life, and fruit has in it *the seeds for more fruit.* Usually it is the *seed* that is sown, but here it is the *fruit* that is sown. As we share the fruit of God with others, they are fed and satisfied, and they in turn bear fruit.

The Christian life is a life of sowing and reaping. For that matter, *every* life is a life of sowing and reaping, and we reap just what we sow. The Christian who obeys God's wisdom sows righteousness, not sin, and peace, not war. The life we live enables the Lord to bring righteousness and peace into the lives of others.

What we *are* is what we live, and what we live is what we sow. What we sow determines what we reap. If we live in God's wisdom, we sow righteousness and peace, and we reap God's blessing. If we live in man's worldly wisdom, we sow sin and war, and we reap "confusion and every evil work."

It is a serious thing to be a troublemaker in God's family. One of the sins that God hates is that of sowing "discord among brethren" (read Prov. 6:16-19). Lot followed the world's wisdom and brought trouble to the camp of Abraham; but Abraham followed God's wisdom and brought peace. Lot's decision led to "good-for-nothing works," and everything he lived for went up in smoke at the destruction of Sodom and Gomorrah. Abraham's decision, in the wisdom of God, led to blessings for his own household and ultimately for the whole world. (Read Gen. 13.)

"Happy is the man that findeth wisdom, and the man that getteth understanding" (Prov. 3:13).

9
How to End Wars

(JAMES 4:1–12)

Have you ever heard of "The War of the Whiskers" or "The War of the Oaken Bucket"? How about "The War of Jenkins' Ear"? These were actual wars fought between nations, and you can read about them in most history books.

War is a fact of life, in spite of treaties, world peace organizations, and the threat of atomic bombs. Not only are there wars between nations, but there are wars of one kind or another on almost every level of life—even "gas wars" among filling station operators!

James discussed this important theme of war in this paragraph, and he explained that there were three wars going on in the world. He also told how these wars could be stopped.

At War with Each Other (4:1, 11-12)

"What causes fights and quarrels among you?" (NIV) Among Christians! "Behold, how good and how pleasant it is for brethren to dwell together in unity" (Ps. 133:1). Surely *brethren* should live together in love and harmony, yet often they do not. Lot caused a quarrel with his Uncle Abraham (Gen. 13). Absalom created a war for his father David (2 Sam. 13—18). Even the disciples created problems for the Lord when they argued over who was the greatest in the kingdom (Luke 9:46-48).

When you examine some of the early churches, you discover that they had their share of disagreements. The members of the Corinthian church were competing with each other in the public meetings, and even suing each other in court (1 Cor. 6:1-8 and 14:23-40). The Galatian believers were "biting and devouring" one another (Gal. 5:15). Paul had to admonish the Ephesians to cultivate spiritual unity (Eph. 4:1-16); and even his beloved church at Philippi had problems: two women could not get along with each other (Phil. 4:1-3).

James mentioned several different kinds of disagreements among the saints.

Class wars (2:1-9). Here is that age-long rivalry between the rich and the poor. The rich man gets the attention, the poor man is ignored. The rich man is honored, the poor man is disgraced. How tragic it is when local churches get their values confused and cater to the rich while they ignore, or even reject, the poor. If fellowship in a church depends on such external things as clothing and economic status, then the church is out of the will of God.

Employment wars (5:1-6). Again, it is the rich man who has the power to control and hurt the poor man. Laborers do not get their wages, or they do not get their fair wages. In spite of our modern labor movement and federal legislation, there are still many people who cannot get a good job, or whose income is less than adequate for the work they are doing.

Church fights (1:19-20, 3:13-18). Apparently, the believers James wrote to were at war with each other over positions in the church, many of them wanting to be teachers and leaders. When they studied the Word, the result was not edification, but strife and arguments. Each person thought that his ideas were the only right ideas and his ways the only right ways. Selfish ambition ruled their meetings, not spiritual submission.

Personal wars (4:11-12). The saints were speaking evil of one another and judging one another. Here, again, we see the wrong use of the tongue. Christians are to speak "the truth in love" (Eph. 4:15); they are not to speak evil in a spirit of rivalry and criticism. If the truth about a brother is harmful, then we should cover it in love and not repeat it (1 Peter 4:8). If he has sinned, we should go to him personally and try to win him back (Matt. 18:15-19; Gal. 6:1-2).

James was not forbidding us to use discrimination or even to evaluate people. Christians need to have discernment (Phil. 1:9-10), but they must not act like God in passing judgment. We must first examine our own lives, and then try to help others (Matt. 7:1-5). We never know all the facts in a case, and we certainly never know the motives that are at work in men's hearts. To speak evil of a brother, and to judge a brother, on the basis of partial evidence and (probably) unkind motives is to sin against him and against God. We are not called to be judges; God is the only Judge. He is patient and understanding; His judgments are just and holy; we can leave the matter with Him.

It is unfortunate that the saints are at war with each other, leader against leader, church against church, fellowship against fellowship. The world watches these religious wars and says, "Behold, how they hate one another!" No wonder Jesus prayed, "That they all may be one; as Thou, Father, art in Me, and I in Thee, that they also may be one in Us; that the world may believe that Thou hast sent Me" (John 17:21).

But, why are we at war with one another? We belong to the same family; we trust the same Saviour; we are indwelt by the same Holy Spirit—and yet we fight one another. Why? James answered this question by explaining the second war that is going on.

At War with Ourselves (4:1b-3)

"What causes fights and quarrels among you? Don't they come from your desires that battle within you?" (James 4:1, NIV) The war in the heart is helping to cause the wars in the church! "But if ye have bitter envying and strife in your hearts, glory not, and lie not against the truth. . . . For where envying and strife is, there is confusion and every evil work" (3:14, 16).

The essence of sin is selfishness. Eve disobeyed God because she wanted to eat of the tree and become wise like God. Abraham lied about his wife because he selfishly wanted to save his own life (Gen. 12:10-20). Achan caused defeat to Israel because he selfishly took some forbidden loot from the ruins of Jericho (Josh. 7). "We have turned every one to his own way" (Isa. 53:6).

Often we veil our religious quarrels under the disguise of "spirituality." We are like Miriam and Aaron who complained about Moses' wife, but who

really were envious of Moses' authority (Num. 12).
Or we imitate James and John who asked for special thrones in the kingdom, when what we really
want is recognition today (Mark 10:35-45). In both
of these instances, the result of selfish desire was
chastening and division among God's people.
Miriam's sin halted the progress of Israel for a
whole week!

Selfish desires are dangerous things. They lead
to *wrong actions* ("ye kill, ye fight and war" James
4:2), and they even lead to *wrong praying* ("When
you ask, you do not receive, because you ask with
wrong motives, that you may spend what you get
on your pleasures" 4:3, NIV). When our praying is
wrong, our whole Christian life is wrong. It has
well been said that the purpose of prayer is not to
get man's will done in heaven, but to get God's will
done on earth.

"Thou shalt not covet" is the last of God's Ten
Commandments, but it's violation can make us
break all of the other nine! Covetousness can make
a person murder, tell lies, dishonor his parents,
commit adultery, and in one way or another violate
all of God's moral law. Selfish living and selfish
praying always lead to war. If there is war on the
inside, there will ultimately be war on the outside.

People who are at war with themselves because
of selfish desires are always unhappy people. They
never enjoy life. Instead of being thankful for the
blessings they do have, they complain about the
blessings they do not have. They cannot get along
with other people because they are always envying
others for what they have and do. They are always
looking for that "magic something" that will change
their lives, when the real problem is within their
own hearts.

Sometimes we use prayer as a cloak to hide our true desires. "But I prayed about it!" can be one of the biggest excuses a Christian can use. Instead of seeking God's will, we tell God what He is supposed to do; and we get angry at Him if He does not obey. This anger at God eventually spills over and we get angry at God's people. More than one church split has been caused by saints who take out their frustrations with God on the members of the church. Many a church or family problem would be solved if people would only look into their own hearts and see the battles raging there.

God made us a unity; mind, emotions, and will should work together. James stated the reason we are at war with ourselves and, consequently, with each other.

At War with God (4:4-10)

The root cause of every war, internal and external, is rebellion against God. At the beginning of creation, you behold perfect harmony; but sin came into the world, and this led to confict. Sin is lawlessness (1 John 3:4), and lawlessness is rebellion against God.

How does a believer declare war against God? By being friendly with God's enemies. James names three enemies that we must not fraternize with if we want to be at peace with God.

The world (4:4). By the "world," James means, of course, human society apart from God. The whole system of things in this society of ours is anti-Christ and anti-God. Abraham was the friend of God (James 2:23); Lot was the friend of the world. Lot ended up in a war, and Abraham had to rescue him (Gen. 14).

A Christian gets involved with the world *grad-*

ually, as I pointed out in Chapter 4 of this study. First, there is "the friendship of the world" (James 4:4). This results in being "spotted" by the world (1:27) so that areas of our lives meet with the approval of the world. Friendship leads to loving the world (1 John 2:15-17), and this makes it easy to conform to the world (Rom. 12:2). The sad result is being condemned with the world (1 Cor. 11:32), our souls saved "yet as by fire" (1 Cor. 3:11-15).

Friendship with the world is compared to adultery. The believer is "married to Christ" (Rom. 7:4) and ought to be faithful to Him. The Jewish Christians who read this letter would understand this picture of "spiritual adultery" because the prophets Ezekiel, Jeremiah, and Hosea used it when rebuking Judah for her sins. (See Jer. 3:1-5; Ezek. 23; and Hosea 1—2.) By adopting the sinful ways of the other nations, and by worshiping their gods, the nation of Judah committed adultery against her God.

The world is the enemy of God, and whoever wills to be a friend of the world cannot be the friend of God. Neither can he be if he lives for the flesh, for this is the second enemy James named.

The flesh (4:1, 5). By "the flesh" is meant the old nature that we inherited from Adam, that is prone to sin. The flesh is not the body. The body is not sinful; the body is neutral. The Spirit may use the body to glorify God, or the flesh may use the body to serve sin. When a sinner yields to Christ, he receives a new nature within, but the old nature is neither removed nor reformed. For this reason, there is a battle within: "For the sinful nature desires what is contrary to the Spirit, and the Spirit what is contrary to the sinful nature. They are in conflict with each other so that you do not do what you want" (Gal. 5:17, NIV). This is what James terms "your lusts that are in your members" (4:1).

Living for the flesh means grieving the Holy Spirit of God who lives in us. "Or do you think Scripture says without reason that the Spirit He caused to live in us longs jealously?" (James 4:5, NIV, margin). Just as the world is the enemy of God the Father, so the flesh is the enemy of God the Holy Spirit. There is a holy, loving jealousy that a husband and wife have over each other, and rightly so. The Spirit within jealously guards our relationship to God, and the Spirit is grieved when we sin against God's love.

Living to please the old nature means to declare war against God. "The carnal mind is enmity against God" (Rom. 8:7). To allow the flesh to control the mind is to lose the blessing of fellowship with God. Abraham had a spiritual mind; he walked with God and enjoyed peace. Lot had a carnal mind; he disobeyed God and experienced war. "For to be carnally minded is death, but to be spiritually minded is life and peace" (Rom. 8:6).

The devil (4:6-7). The world is in conflict with the Father; the flesh fights against the Holy Spirit; and the devil opposes the Son of God. Pride is Satan's great sin, and it is one of his chief weapons in his warfare against the saint and the Saviour. God wants us to be humble; Satan wants us to be proud. "Ye shall be as God," Satan promised Eve, and she believed him. A new Christian must not be put into places of spiritual leadership "lest being lifted up with pride he fall into the condemnation of the devil" (1 Tim. 3:6).

God wants us to depend on His grace ("But He giveth more grace"), while the devil wants us to depend on ourselves. Satan is the author of all "do-it-yourself" spiritual enterprises. He enjoys inflating the ego and encouraging the believer to do it his own way. In spite of Jesus' warnings about Satan's plans, Peter fell into the snare, pulled out his sword, and tried to accomplish God's will in his own way. What a mess he made of things!

One of the problems in our churches today is that we have too many celebrities and not enough servants. Christian workers are promoted so much that there is very little place left for God's glory. Man has nothing to be proud of in himself. There dwells no good thing in us (Rom. 7:18); but when we trust Christ, He puts that "good thing" in us that makes us His children (2 Tim. 1:6, 14).

Here, then, are three enemies that want to turn us away from God: the world, the flesh, and the devil. These enemies are left over from our old life of sin (Eph. 2:1-3). Christ has delivered us from them, but they still attack us. How can we overcome them? How can we be the friends of God and the enemies of the world, the flesh, and the devil? James gives us three instructions to follow if we would enjoy peace instead of war.

Submit to God (4:7). This word is a military term that means "get into your proper rank." When a buck private acts like the general, there is going to be trouble! Unconditional surrender is the only way to complete victory. If there is any area of the life kept back from God, there will always be battles. This explains why uncommitted Christians cannot live with themselves or with other people.

"Neither give place to the devil," cautions Paul in Ephesians 4:27. Satan needs a foothold in our lives if he is going to fight against God; and *we give him that foothold.* The way to resist the devil is to submit to God.

After King David committed adultery with Bath-sheba, and killed her husband, he hid his sins for almost a year. There was war between him and God, and David had declared it. Read Psalms 32 and 51 to discover the high price David paid to be at war with God. When he finally submitted to God, David experienced peace and joy. This too he recorded in Psalms 32 and 51. Submission is an act of the will; it is saying, "Not my will but Thine be done."

Draw near to God (4:8). How do we do this? By confessing our sins and asking for His cleansing. "Cleanse your hands, ye sinners; and purify your hearts, ye double-minded." The Greek word translated *purify* means "make chaste." This parallels the idea of "spiritual adultery" in verse 4.

Dr. A. W. Tozer has a profound essay in one of his books, entitled, "Nearness is Likeness." The more we are like God, the nearer we are to God. I may be sitting in my living room with my Siamese cat on my lap, and my wife may be 20 feet away in the kitchen; yet I am nearer to my wife than to the cat because the cat is unlike me. We have very little in common.

God graciously draws near to us when we deal with the sin in our lives that keeps Him at a distance. He will not share us with anyone else; He must have complete control. The double-minded Christian can never be close to God. Again, Abraham and Lot come to mind. Abraham "drew near" and talked to God about Sodom (Gen. 18:23ff), while Lot moved into Sodom and lost the blessing of God.

Humble yourselves before God (4:9-10). It is possible to submit outwardly and yet not be humbled inwardly. God hates the sin of pride (Prov.

6:16-17), and He will chasten the proud believer until he is humbled. We have a tendency to treat sin too lightly, even to laugh about it ("let your laughter be turned into mourning"). But sin is serious, and one mark of true humility is facing the seriousness of sin and dealing with our disobedience. "A broken and a contrite heart, O God, Thou wilt not despise" (Ps. 51:17).

Sometimes we hear a believer pray, "O Lord, humble me!" That is a dangerous thing to pray. Far better that we humble ourselves before God, confess our sins, weep over them, and turn from them. "To this man will I look, even to him that is poor and of a contrite spirit, and trembleth at My Word" (Isa. 66:2). "The Lord is nigh unto them that are of a broken heart; and saveth such as be of a contrite spirit" (Ps. 34:18).

If we obey these three instructions, then God will draw near, cleanse us, and forgive us; *and the wars will cease!* We will not be at war with God, so we will not be at war with ourselves. This means we will not be at war with others. "And the work of righteousness shall be peace; and the effect of righteousness quietness and assurance forever" (Isa. 32:17).

Put the government of your life upon His shoulders, and let Him become the Prince of Peace (Isa. 9:6).

10

Plan Ahead

(JAMES 4:13–17)

James began chapter 4 talking about war with
God, and he ends it talking about the will of God.
But the two themes are related: when a believer is
out of the will of God, he becomes a troublemaker
and not a peacemaker.

Lot moved into Sodom and brought trouble to
his family. David committed adultery and brought
trouble to his family and his kingdom. Jonah disobeyed God and almost sent a shipload of heathen
sailors into a watery grave. In each case, there was
a wrong attitude toward the will of God.

That God would have a plan for each of our lives
is an obvious truth. He is a God of *wisdom* and
knows what ought to happen and when it should
occur. And, as a God of *love,* He must desire the
very best for His children. Too many Christians
look upon the will of God as bitter medicine they
must take, instead of seeing it as the gracious evidence of the love of God.

"I would give my life to the Lord, but I'm afraid," a perplexed teenager told me at a church youth conference.

"What are you afraid of?" I asked.

"I'm afraid God will ask me to do something dangerous!"

"The dangerous life is not *in* the will of God," I replied, "but *out of* the will of God. The safest place in the world is right where God wants you."

I was going through a difficult time in my own ministry some years ago, questioning the will of God. While on vacation, I was reading the Book of Psalms, asking God to give me some assurance and encouragement. Psalm 33:11 was the answer to that prayer: "The counsel of the Lord standeth forever; the thoughts of His heart to all generations."

"The *will* of God comes from the *heart* of God," I said to myself. "His will is the expression of His love, so I don't have to be afraid!" It was a turning point in my life to discover the blessing of loving and living the will of God.

In this section of his letter, James pointed out three attitudes toward the will of God. Of course, only one of them is the correct one, the one that every Christian ought to cultivate.

Ignoring God's Will (4:13-14, 16)

Perhaps James was addressing the wealthy merchants in the assembly. They might have discussed their business deals and boasted about their plans. There is no evidence that they sought the will of God or prayed about their decisions. They measured success in life by how many times they got their own way and accomplished what they had planned.

But James presented four arguments that revealed the foolishness of ignoring the will of God.

The complexity of life (4:13). Think of all that is involved in life: today, tomorrow, buying, selling, getting gain, losing, going here, going there. Life is made up of people and places, activities and goals, days and years; and each of us must make many crucial decisions day after day.

Apart from the will of God, life is a mystery. When you know Jesus Christ as your Saviour, and seek to do His will, then life starts to make sense. Even the physical world around you takes on new meaning. There is a simplicity and unity to your life that makes for poise and confidence. You are no longer living in a mysterious, threatening universe. You can sing, "This is my Father's world!"

The uncertainty of life (4:14a). This statement is based on Proverbs 27:1—"Boast not thyself of tomorrow; for thou knowest not what a day may bring forth." These businessmen were making plans for a whole year when they could not even see ahead into *one day!* See how confident they were: "We will go. We will stay a year. We will buy and sell and make a profit."

Their attitude reminds us of the farmer in the parable of Jesus in Luke 12:16-21. The man had a bumper crop; his barns were too small; so he decided to build bigger barns and have greater security for the future. "And I will say to my soul, 'Soul, thou hast much goods laid up for many years; take thine ease, eat, drink, and be merry'" (v. 19).

What was God's reply to this man's boasting? "Thou fool, this night thy soul shall be required of thee" (v. 20). Life is not uncertain to God, but it is uncertain to us. Only when we are in His will can we be confident of tomorrow, for we know that He is leading us.

The brevity of life (4:14b). This is one of the repeated themes of Scripture. To us, life seems long and we measure it in years; but in comparison to eternity, life is but a vapor. James borrowed that figure from the Book of Job where you find many pictures of the brevity of life.

"My days are swifter than a weaver's shuttle" (Job 7:6). "The cloud is consumed and vanisheth away" (7:9). "Our days upon earth are a shadow" (8:9). "Now my days are swifter than a post" (9:25), referring to the royal couriers that hastened in their missions. "They are passed away as the swift ships: as the eagle that hasteth to the prey" (9:26). "Man that is born of a woman is of few days, and full of trouble. He cometh forth like a flower, and is cut down: he fleeth also as a shadow, and continueth not" (14:1-2).

We count our *years* at each birthday, but God tells us to number our *days* (Ps. 90:12). After all, we live a day at a time, and those days rush by quickly the older we grow.

Since life is so brief, we cannot afford merely to "spend our lives"; and we certainly do not want to "waste our lives." We must *invest our lives* in those things that are eternal.

God reveals His will in His Word, and yet most people ignore the Bible. In the Bible, God gives precepts, principles, and promises that can guide us in every area of life. Knowing and obeying the Word of God is the surest way to success (Josh. 1:8 and Ps. 1:3.)

The frailty of man (4:16). "As it is, you boast and brag. All such boasting is evil" (NIV). Man's boasting only covers up man's weakness. "Man proposes but God disposes," wrote Thomas à Kempis. Solomon said it first: "The lot is cast into the lap: but the whole disposing thereof is of the Lord" (Prov. 16:33). Man cannot control future events. He has neither the wisdom to *see* the future nor the power to *control* the future. For him to boast is sin; it is making himself God.

How foolish it is for people to ignore the will of God. It is like going through the dark jungles without a map, or over the stormy seas without a compass. When we visited Mammoth Cave in Kentucky, I was impressed with the maze of tunnels and the dense darkness when the lights were turned off. When we got to the "Pulpit Rock," the man in charge of the tour gave a five-word sermon from it: "Stay close to your guide." Good counsel indeed!

Disobeying God's Will (4:17)

These people *know* the will of God but choose to disobey it. This attitude expresses even more pride than does the first; for the person says to God, "I know what You want me to do, but I prefer not to do it. I really know more about this than You do!" "For it had been better for them not to have known the way of righteousness, than, after they have known it, to turn from the holy commandment delivered unto them" (2 Peter 2:21).

Why do people who know the will of God deliberately disobey it? I have already suggested one reason: pride. Man likes to boast that he is the "master of his fate, the captain of his soul." Man has accomplished so many marvelous things that he thinks he can do anything.

Another reason is man's ignorance of the nature of God's will. He acts as though the will of God is something he can accept or reject. In reality, the will of God is not an option; it is an obligation. We cannot "take it or leave it." Because He is the

Creator and we are the creatures, we must obey Him. Because He is the Saviour and Lord, and we are His children and servants, we must obey Him. To treat the will of God lightly is to invite the chastening of God in our lives.

Many people have the mistaken idea that the will of God is a formula for misery. Just the opposite is true! It is *disobeying* the Lord's will that leads to misery. The Bible, and human experience, are both witnesses to this truth. And even if a disobedient Christian seems to escape difficulty in this life, what will he say when he faces the Lord? "And that servant which knew his lord's will, and prepared not himself, neither did according to his will, shall be beaten with many stripes. But he that knew not, and did commit things worthy of stripes, shall be beaten with few stripes" (Luke 12:47-48).

What happens to Christians who deliberately disobey the known will of God? They are chastened by their loving Father until they submit (Heb. 12:5-11). If a professed believer is not chastened, it is evidence that he has never truly been born again but is a counterfeit. God's chastening is an evidence of His love, not His hatred. Just as we earthly fathers spank our children to help them respect our will and obey, so our heavenly Father chastens His own. Though chastening is hard to take, it has a comforting truth of sonship with it.

But there is also the danger of losing heavenly rewards. In 1 Corinthians 9:24-27, Paul compared the believer to a runner in the Greek races. In order to qualify for a crown, he had to obey the rules of the game. If any contestant was found to have disobeyed the rules, he was disqualified and humiliated. The word "castaway" in 1 Corinthians 9:27 does not refer to the loss of salvation, but the loss of reward. "Disqualified" would be a good translation.

Disobeying God's will today may not seem a serious thing, but it will appear very serious when the Lord returns and examines our works (Col. 3:22-25).

Obeying God's Will (4:15)

"If the Lord will" is not just a statement on a believer's lips: it is the constant attitude of his heart. "My food," said Jesus, "is to do the will of Him who sent Me and to finish His work" (John 4:34). Often in his letters, Paul referred to the will of God as he shared his plans with his friends (Rom. 1:10; 15:32; 1 Cor. 4:19; 16:7). Paul did not consider the will of God a chain that shackled him; rather, it was a key that opened doors and set him free.

Everything in this universe operates according to laws. If we cooperate with these laws and obey them, then the universe works *with* us. But if we fight these laws and disobey them, the universe will work *against* us. For example, certain laws govern flight. The engineer who obeys those laws in designing and building the plane, and the pilot who obeys those laws in flying the plane, will both have the joy of seeing the great machine operate perfectly. But if they disobey the basic laws that govern flight, the result will be a crash and the loss of life and money.

God's will for our lives is comparable to the laws He has built within the universe, with this exception: those laws are general, but the will He has planned for our lives is specifically designed for us. No two lives are planned according to the same pattern.

To be sure, there are some things that must be

true of all Christians. It is God's will that we yield
ourselves to Him (2 Cor. 8:5). It is God's will that
we avoid sexual immorality (1 Thes. 4:3). All Christians should rejoice, pray, and thank God (1 Thes.
5:16-18). Every commandment in the Bible addressed to believers is part of the will of God, and
must be obeyed. But God does not call each of us
to the same work in life, or to exercise the same
gifts and ministry. The will of God is "tailor-made"
for each of us!

It is important that we have the right attitude
toward the will of God. Some people think God's
will is a cold, impersonal machine. God starts it
going and it is up to us to keep it functioning
smoothly. If we disobey Him in some way, the machine grinds to a halt, and we are out of God's will
for the rest of our lives.

God's will is not a cold, impersonal machine.
You do not determine God's will in some mechan-
ical way, like getting a soft drink out of a "pop"
machine. *The will of God is a living relationship
between God and the believer.* This relationship is
not *destroyed* when the believer disobeys, for the
Father still deals with His child, even if He must
chasten.

Rather than looking at the will of God as a cold,
impersonal machine, I prefer to see it as a warm,
growing, living body. If something goes wrong
with my body, I don't die: the other parts of the
body compensate for it until I get that organ working properly again. There is pain; there is also
weakness; but there is not necessarily death.

When you and I get out of God's will, it is not
the end of everything. We suffer, to be sure; but
when God cannot rule, He overrules. Just as the
body compensates for the malfunctioning of one

part, so God adjusts things to bring us back into his will. You see this illustrated clearly in the lives of Abraham and Jonah.

The believer's relationship to the will of God is a growing experience. First, we should *know His will* (Acts 22:14). The will of God is not difficult to discover. If we are willing to obey, He is willing to reveal (John 7:17). It has been said that "obedience is the organ of spiritual knowledge." This is true. God does not reveal His will to the curious or the careless, but to those who are ready and willing to obey Him.

But we must not stop with merely knowing *some* of God's will. God wants us to be "filled with the knowledge of His will and all wisdom and spiritual understanding" (Col. 1:9). It is wrong to want to know God's will about some matters and ignore His will in other matters. Everything in our lives is important to God, and He has a plan for each detail.

God wants us to *understand His will* (Eph. 5:17). This is where spiritual wisdom comes in. A child can *know* the will of his father, but he may not *understand* his will. The child knows the "what" but not the "why." As the "friends" of Jesus Christ, we have the privilege of knowing why God does what He does (John 15:15). "He made known His ways unto Moses, His acts unto the children of Israel" (Ps. 103:7). The Israelites knew *what* God was doing, but Moses understood *why* He was doing it.

We must also *prove God's will* (Rom. 12:2). The Greek verb means "to prove by experience." We learn to determine the will of God by working at it. The more we obey, the easier it is to discover what God wants us to do. It is something like learning to

swim or play a musical instrument. You eventually
"get the feel" of what you are doing, and it becomes
second nature to you.

People who keep asking, "How do I determine
God's will for my life?" are announcing to everybody that they have never really tried to do God's
will. You start with the thing you know you ought
to do, and you do that. Then God opens the way
for the next step. You prove by experience what
the will of God is. We learn both from successes
and failures. "Take My yoke upon you, and learn of
Me" (Matt. 11:29). The yoke suggests doing things
together, putting into practice what God has taught
you.

Finally, we must *do God's will from the heart*
(Eph. 6:6). Jonah knew the will of God, and (after
a spanking) did the will of God; but he did not do
it from his heart. Jonah 4 indicates that the angry
prophet did not love the Lord, nor did he love the
people of Nineveh. He merely did God's will to
keep from getting another spanking!

What Paul said about giving can also be applied
to living: "not grudgingly, or of necessity, for God
loveth a cheerful giver" (2 Cor. 9:7). *Grudgingly*
means "reluctantly, painfully." They get absolutely
no joy out of doing God's will. *Of necessity* means
"under compulsion." These people obey because
they have to, not because they want to. Their heart
is not in it.

The secret of a happy life is to delight in duty.
When duty becomes delight, then burdens become
blessings. "Thy statutes have been my songs in the
house of my pilgrimage" (Ps. 119:54). When we
love God, then His statutes become songs, and we
enjoy serving Him. When we serve God grudgingly, or because we have to, we may accomplish

His work but we ourselves will miss the blessing. It will be toil, not ministry. But when we do God's will from the heart, we are enriched, no matter how difficult the task might have been.

We must never think that a failure in knowing or doing God's will permanently affects our relationship with the Lord. We can confess our sins and receive His forgiveness (1 John 1:9). We can learn from the mistakes. The important thing is a heart that loves God and wants sincerely to do His will and glorify His name.

What are the benefits of doing the will of God? For one thing, you enjoy a deeper fellowship with Jesus Christ (Mark 3:35). You have the privilege of knowing God's truth (John 7:17) and seeing your prayers answered (1 John 5:14-15). There is an eternal quality to the life and works of the one who does the will of God (1 John 2:15-17). Certainly, there is the expectation of reward at the return of Jesus Christ (Matt. 25:34).

Which of these three attitudes do you have toward the will of God? Do you totally ignore God's will as you make your daily plans and decisions? Or, do you know God's will and yet refuse to obey it? Each attitude is wrong and can only bring sorrow and ruin to the life of the person who holds it.

But the Christian who knows, loves, and obeys the will of God will enjoy God's blessing. His life may not be easier, but it will be holier and happier. His very food will be the will of God (John 4:34); it will be the joy and delight of his heart (Ps. 40:8).

11

Money Talks

(JAMES 5:1–6)

"If money talks," said a popular comedian, "all it ever says to me is good-bye!"

But money was not saying "good-bye" to the men James addressed in this section of his letter. These men were rich, and their riches were sinful. They were using their wealth for selfish purposes, and were persecuting the poor in the process.

One of the themes that runs through James 5 is *trouble*. We meet poor people deprived of their wages (5:4), as well as people who are physically afflicted (5:13-16), and spiritually backslidden (5:19-20). A second theme that James introduced is *prayer*. The poor laborers cry out to God (5:4). The sick and afflicted should pray (5:13-16). He cited Elijah as an example of one who believed in prayer (5:17-18).

When you join these two themes, you arrive at the fifth mark of the mature Christian: *he is prayerful in troubles*. Instead of giving up when troubles come, the mature believer turns to God in prayer and seeks divine help. The immature person trusts in his own experience and skill, or else turns to others for help. While it is true that God often meets our needs through the hands of other people, this aid must be the result of prayer.

James did not say it was a sin to be rich. After all, Abraham was a wealthy man, yet he walked with God, and was greatly used of God to bless the whole world. James was concerned about the selfishness of the rich, and advised them to "weep and howl." He gave three reasons for his exhortation.

The Way They Got Their Wealth (5:4 and 6a)

The Bible does not discourage the acquiring of wealth. In the Law of Moses, specific rules are laid down for getting and securing wealth. The Jews in Canaan owned their own property, worked it, and benefited from the produce. In several of His parables, Jesus indicated His respect for personal property and private gain. There is nothing in the Epistles that contradicts the right of private ownership and profit.

What the Bible does condemn is acquiring wealth by illegal means or for illegal purposes. The Prophet Amos thundered a message of judgment against the wealthy upper crust who robbed the poor and used their stolen wealth for selfish luxuries. Isaiah and Jeremiah also exposed the selfishness of the rich and warned that judgment was coming. It is in this spirit that James wrote. He gave two illustrations of how the rich acquired their wealth.

Holding back wages (5:4). Laborers were hired and paid by the day and did not have any legal

contracts with their employers. The parable of the
laborers in Matthew 20:1-16 gives some idea of the
system in that day. In the Law, God gave definite
instructions concerning the laboring man in order
to protect him from the oppressive employer.

"You shall not oppress a hired servant who is
poor and needy, whether he is one of your countrymen or one of your aliens who is in your land in
your towns. You shall give him his wages on his
day before the sun sets, for he is poor and sets his
heart on it; so that he may not cry against you to
the Lord and it become sin in you" (Deut. 24:14-15,
NASB).

"You shall not oppress your neighbor, nor rob
him. The wages of a hired man are not to remain
with you all night until morning" (Lev. 19:13,
NASB).

"Woe to him that buildeth his house by unrigh-
teousness, and his chambers by wrong; that useth
his neighbor's service without wages, and giveth
him not for his work" (Jer. 22:13).

These rich men had hired the laborers and promised to pay them a specific amount. The men had
completed their work but had not been paid. The
tense of the verb "kept back" in the original Greek
indicates that the laborers *never will get their
salaries.*

"Thou shalt not steal" is still the law of God, and
it is a law He will enforce. As Christians, it be-
hooves us to be faithful to pay our bills. As a pastor,
I find myself embarrassed when unsaved men tell
me about Christians who owe them money and apparently have no intention of paying.

I recall meeting a doctor friend while I was visiting in the hospital. "How are things going?" I
asked, and he replied, "Oh, I guess things are OK."

"I pray for you," I told him, wanting to be an encouragement.

"I appreciate that," he replied. "But while you're at it, pray for all the people who owe me money. It'd help if they would pay up!"

Controlling the courts (5:6a). It is often the case that those who have wealth also have political power and can get what they want. "What is the Golden Rule?" asked a character in a comic strip. His friend answered, "Whoever has the gold makes the rules!" James asked, "Do not the rich men oppress you and draw you before the judgment seats?" (2:6)

When the name *Watergate* is mentioned, nobody thinks of a beautiful hotel. That word reminds us of an ugly episode in American history that led to the revelation of lies and the resignation of the President of the United States. Each side accused the other of obstructing justice and manipulating the laws.

When God established Israel in her land, He gave the people a system of courts. (See Deut. 17:8-13). He warned the judges not to be greedy (Ex. 18:21). They were not to be partial to the rich or the poor (Lev. 19:15). No judge was to tolerate perjury (Deut. 19:16-21). Bribery was condemned by the Lord (Isa. 33:15; Micah 3:11; 7:3). The Prophet Amos denounced the judges in his day who took bribes and "fixed" cases (Amos 5:12, 15).

The courts in James' day were apparently easy to control if you had enough money. The poor workers could not afford expensive lawsuits, so they were beaten down every time. The workers had the just cause, but they were not given justice. Instead, they were abused and ruined. ("Killed" should probably be taken in a figurative way, as

in James 4:2, although it is possible that the rich
men could so oppress the poor that the poor would
die.) The poor man did not resist the rich man
because he had no weapons with which to fight.
All he could do was call on the Lord for justice.

The Bible warns us against the securing of
wealth by illegal means. God owns all wealth (Ps.
50:10); He permits us to be stewards of His wealth
for His glory. "Wealth obtained by fraud dwindles,
but the one who gathers by labor increases it"
(Prov. 13:11, NASB). It is "the hand of the diligent
that makes rich" (Prov. 10:4). "Do not weary yourself to gain wealth" (Prov. 23:4). We must put God
first in our lives, and He will see to it that we
always have all that we need (Matt. 6:33). .

The Way the Rich Used Their Wealth (5:3-5)

It is bad enough to gain wealth in a sinful way,
but to use that wealth in sinful ways just makes the
sin greater.

They stored it up (5:3). Of course, there is nothing sinful about saving. "For the children ought
not to lay up for the parents, but the parents for
the children" (2 Cor. 12:14). "But if any provide
not for his own, and specially for those of his own
house, he hath denied the faith, and is worse than
an infidel" (1 Tim. 5:8). "Then you ought to have
put my money in the bank, and on my arrival I
would have received my money back with interest"
(Matt. 25:27, NASB).

But it is wrong to store up wealth when you
owe money to your employees. These rich men
were hoarding grain, gold, and garments. They
thought that they were rich because they had these
possessions. Instead of laying up treasures in heaven
by using their wealth for God's glory (Matt.

6:19ff.), they were selfishly guarding it for their own security and pleasure. Not more than 10 years after James wrote this letter, Jerusalem fell to the Romans, and all this accumulated wealth was taken.

What did Jesus mean by "laying up treasures in heaven"? Did He mean we should "sell everything and give to the poor" as He instructed the rich young ruler? I think not. He spoke that way to the rich ruler because covetousness was the young man's besetting sin, and Jesus wanted to expose it. To lay up treasures in heaven means to use all that we have as stewards of God's wealth. You and I may *possess* many things, but we do not *own* them. God is the Owner of everything, and we are His stewards.

What we possess and use are merely things, apart from the will of God. When we yield to His will and use what He gives us to serve Him, then things become treasures and we are investing in eternity. What we do on earth is recorded in heaven, and God keeps the books and pays the interest.

What a tragedy it is to see people "heap up treasures for the last days" instead of "laying up treasures in heaven." The Bible does not discourage saving, or even investing; but it does condemn hoarding.

They kept others from benefiting from it (5:4). By fraudulent means, the rich men robbed the poor. The rich men were not using their own wealth, but they would not pay their laborers and permit them to use the wealth. Perhaps they were waiting for salaries to go down.

Since we are stewards of God's wealth, we have certain responsibilities toward our Master. We must be faithful to use what He gives us for the good of others and the glory of God. "Moreover, it is required in stewards, that a man be found faithful" (1 Cor. 4:2). Joseph was a faithful steward in Potiphar's house, and Potiphar prospered. There are ways that we can use God's wealth to help others.

They lived in luxury (5:5). "You have lived in high style on the earth!" (James 5:5, literal translation) Luxury is waste, and waste is sin.

A magazine advertisement told of the shopping spree of an oil-rich Sultan. He purchased 19 Cadillacs, one for each of his 19 wives, and paid extra to have the cars lengthened. He also bought two Porsches, six Mercedes, a $40,000 speedboat and a truck for hauling it. Add to the list 16 refrigerators, $47,000 worth of women's luggage, two Florida grapefruit trees, two reclining chairs, and one slot machine. His total bill was $1,500,000, and he had to pay another $194,500 to have everything delivered. Talk about living in luxury!

All of us are grateful for the good things of life, and we would certainly not want to return to primitive conditions. But we recognize the fact that there is a point of diminishing returns. "Tell me what thou dost need," said the Quaker to his neighbor, "and I will tell thee how to get along without it." Jesus said, "Beware and be on your guard against every form of greed; for not even when one has an abundance does his life consist of his possessions" (Luke 12:15, NASB). These rich men James addressed were feeding themselves on their riches and starving to death. The Greek word pictures cattle being fattened for the slaughter.

There is a great difference between enjoying what God has given us (1 Tim. 6:17) and living extravagantly on what we have withheld from others. Even if what we have has been earned lawfully and in the will of God, we must not waste it on selfish living. There are too many needs to be met.

Luxury has a way of ruining character. It is a form of self-indulgence. If you match character with wealth, you can produce much good; but if you match self-indulgence with wealth, the result is sin. The rich man Jesus described in Luke 16:19-31 would have felt right at home with the rich men James wrote to!

What Their Riches Will Do (5:1-4)

The rich thought they had it made because of their wealth, but God thought otherwise. "Howl for your miseries that shall come upon you" (5:1b). James described the consequences of misusing riches.

Riches will vanish (5:2-3a). Grain will rot ("corrupted" in v. 2); gold will rust; and garments will become moth-eaten. Nothing material in this world will last forever. The seeds of death and decay are found in all of creation.

It is a great mistake to think there is security in wealth. Paul wrote, "Instruct those who are rich in this present world not to be conceited, or to fix their hope on the uncertainty of riches" (1 Tim. 6:17). Riches are uncertain. The money market fluctuates from hour to hour, and so does the stock market. Actually, gold does not rust the way iron does; but the idea is the same: the gold is losing its value. Add to this the fact that life is brief, and we cannot take wealth with us, and you can see how foolish it is to live for the things of this world. God said to the rich man, "Thou fool, this night thy soul shall be required of thee: then whose

shall those things be, which thou hast provided?"
(Luke 12:20)

Misused riches erode character (5:3). "Their
corrosion . . . will eat your flesh like fire" (5:3,
NIV). This is a present judgment: the poison of
wealth has infected them and they are being eaten
alive. Of itself, money is not sinful; it is neutral.
But "the love of money is the root of all evil"
(1 Tim. 6:10). "Thou shalt not covet" is the last of
the Ten Commandments, but it is the most dangerous. Covetousness will make a person break all the
other nine Commandments.

Abraham was a rich man, but he maintained his
faith and character. When Lot became rich, it
ruined his character and ultimately ruined his family. It is good to have riches in your hand provided
they do not get into your heart. "If riches increase,
set not your heart upon them" (Ps. 62:10). "A good
name is rather to be chosen than great riches, and
loving favor rather than silver and gold" (Prov.
22:1).

Judgment is a certainty (5:3, 5). James not only
saw a *present* judgment (their wealth decaying,
their character eroding), but also a *future* judgment before God. Jesus Christ will be the Judge
(5:9), and His judgment will be righteous.

Note the witnesses that God will call on that
day of judgment. First, the rich men's *wealth* will
witness against them (5:3). Their rotten grain,
rusted gold and silver, and moth-eaten garments
will bear witness of the selfishness of their hearts.
There is a bit of irony here: the rich men saved
their wealth to help them, but their hoarded riches
will only testify against them.

The *wages* they held back will also witness
against them in court (5:4a). Money talks! These

stolen salaries cry out to God for justice and judgment. God heard Abel's blood cry out from the ground (Gen. 4:10), and He hears this stolen money cry out too.

The *workers* will also testify against them (5:4). There will be no opportunities for the rich to bribe the witnesses or the Judge. God hears the cries of His oppressed people and He will judge righteously.

This judgment is a serious thing. The lost will stand before Christ at the Great White Throne (Rev. 20:11-15). The saved will stand before the judgment seat of Christ (Rom. 14:10-12; 2 Cor. 5:9-10). God will not judge our *sins,* because they have already been judged on the Cross; but He will judge our *works* and our ministry. If we have been faithful in serving and glorifying Him, we will receive a reward; if we have been unfaithful, we shall lose our reward but not our salvation (1 Cor. 3:1-15).

The loss of a precious opportunity (5:3). "The last days" indicates that James believed that the coming of the Lord was near. (See 5:8-9.) We must "buy up the opportunity" (Eph. 5:16, literal translation) and work while it is day (John 9:4). Think of the good that could have been accomplished with that hoarded wealth. There were poor people in that congregation who could have been helped (James 2:1-6). There were workers who deserved their wages. Sad to say, in a few years the Jewish nation was defeated and scattered, and Jerusalem destroyed.

It is good to have the things that money can buy, provided you also have the things that money cannot buy. What good is a $500,000 house if there is no home? Or a million-dollar diamond ring if there is no love? James did not condemn riches or rich people; he condemned the wrong use of riches, and rich people who use their wealth as a weapon and not as a tool with which to build.

It is possible to be "poor in this world" (2:5) and yet rich in the next world. It is also possible to be "rich in this world" (1 Tim. 6:17) and poor in the next world. The return of Jesus Christ will make some people poor and others rich, depending on the spiritual condition of their hearts. "For where your treasure is, there will your heart be also" (Matt. 6:21).

What we keep, we lose. What we give to God, we keep, and He adds interest to it. A famous preacher, known for his long sermons, was asked to give the annual "charity sermon" for the poor. It was suggested that if he preached too long, the congregation might not give as much as they should.

The preacher read his text from Proverbs 19:17—"He that hath pity upon the poor lendeth unto the Lord; and that which he hath given will He pay him again." His sermon indeed was brief:

"If you like the terms, then put down your money."

Yes, money talks. What will it say to you at the last judgment?

12

The Power of Patience

(JAMES 5:7–12)

James was still addressing the suffering saints when he wrote, "Be patient." This was his counsel at the beginning of his letter (1:1-5), and his counsel as his letter came to a close. God is not going to right all the wrongs in this world until Jesus Christ returns, and we believers must patiently endure—and expect.

Three times James reminds us of the coming of the Lord (5:7, 8, and 9). This is the "blessed hope" of the Christian (Titus 2:13). We do not expect to have everything easy and comfortable in this present life. "In the world ye shall have tribulation" (John 16:33). Paul exhorted his converts that "we must through much tribulation enter into the kingdom of God" (Acts 14:22). We must patiently endure hardships and heartaches until Jesus returns.

James used two different words for patience. In verses 7, 8, and 10 it was the word "longtempered." The words "endure" and "patience" in verse 11 literally mean "to remain under" and speak of endurance under great stress. *Patience* means "to stay put and stand fast when you'd like to run away." Many Greek scholars think that "long-suffering" refers to patience with respect to persons, while "endurance" refers to patience with respect to conditions or situations.

But the question we must answer is: How can we as Christians experience this kind of patient endurance as we wait for the Lord to return? To answer that question (and need), James gave three encouraging examples of patient endurance.

The Farmer (5:7-9)

If a man is impatient, then he had better not become a farmer. No crop appears overnight (except perhaps a crop of weeds), and no farmer has control over the weather. Too much rain can cause the crop to rot, and too much sun can burn it up. An early frost can kill the crop. How long-suffering the farmer must be with the weather!

He must also have patience with the seed and the crop, for it takes time for plants to grow. Jewish farmers would plow and sow in what to us are the autumn months. The "early rain" would soften the soil. The "latter rain" would come in the early spring (our February-March) and help to mature the harvest. The farmer had to wait many weeks for his seed to produce fruit.

Why did he willingly wait so long? Because the fruit is "precious" (5:7). The harvest is worth waiting for. "In due season we shall reap, if we faint not" (Gal. 6:9). "For the earth produces crops by itself; first the blade, then the head, then the mature grain in the head. But when the crop permits, he immediately puts in the sickle, because the harvest has come" (Mark 4:28-29, NASB).

James pictured the Christian as a "spiritual farmer" looking for a spiritual harvest. "Be ye also patient, stablish your hearts . . ." (5:8). Our hearts are the soil, and the "seed is the Word of God" (Luke 8:11). There are seasons to the spiritual life just as there are seasons to the soil. Sometimes, our hearts become cold and "wintry," and the Lord has to "plow them up" before He can plant the seed (Jer. 4:3). He sends the sunshine and the rains of His goodness to water and nurture the seeds planted; but we must be patient to wait for the harvest.

Here, then, is a secret of endurance when the going is tough: *God is producing a harvest in our lives.* He wants the "fruit of the Spirit" to grow (Gal. 5:22-23), and the only way He can do it is through trials and troubles. Instead of growing impatient with God and with ourselves, we must yield to the Lord and permit the fruit to grow. We are "spiritual farmers" looking for a harvest.

You can enjoy this kind of a harvest only if your heart is *established* (James 5:8). One of the purposes of the spiritual ministry of the local church is to establish the heart (Rom. 1:11). Paul sent Timothy to Thessalonica to establish the young Christians in their faith (1 Thes. 3:1-3); and Paul also prayed for them that they might be established (1 Thes. 3:10-13). The ministry of the Word of God and prayer are important if the heart is going to be established. A heart that is not established cannot bear fruit.

Keep in mind that the farmer does not stand around doing nothing: he is constantly at work as he looks toward the harvest. James did not tell these suffering believers to put on white robes, climb a hill, and wait for Jesus to return. "Keep working and waiting" was His admonition. "Blessed is that servant, whom his Lord when He cometh shall find so doing" (Luke 12:43).

Nor does the farmer get into fights with his neighbors. One of the usual marks of farmers is their willingness to help one another. Nobody on the farm has time or energy for disputes with the neighbors. James must have had this in mind when he added, "Don't grumble against each other, brothers, or you will be judged" (5:9, NIV). Impatience with God often leads to impatience with God's people, and this is a sin we must avoid. If we start using the sickles on each other, we will miss the harvest!

The Prophets (5:10)

A Jewish congregation would understand this simple reference that James made to the Old Testament prophets. In His Sermon on the Mount, Jesus also used the prophets as an example of victory over persecution (Matt. 5:10-12). What encouragements do we receive from their example?

For one thing, they were in the will of God, yet they suffered. They were preaching "in the name of the Lord," yet they were persecuted. Satan tells the faithful Christian that his suffering is the result of sin or unfaithfulness; and yet his suffering might well be *because of faithfulness!* "Yea, and all that will live godly in Christ Jesus shall suffer persecution" (2 Tim. 3:12). We must never think that obedience automatically produces ease and pleasure. Our Lord was obedient, and it led to a Cross!

The prophets encourage us by reminding us that

God cares for us when we go through sufferings for His sake. Elijah announced to wicked King Ahab that there would be a drought in the land for three and one-half years; and Elijah himself had to suffer in that drought. But God cared for him, and God gave him victory over the evil priests of Baal. It has been said, "The will of God will never lead you where the grace of God cannot keep you."

Many of the prophets had to endure great trials and sufferings, not only at the hands of unbelievers, but at the hands of professed believers. Jeremiah was arrested as a traitor and even thrown into an abandoned well to die. God fed Jeremiah and protected him throughout that terrible siege of Jerusalem, even though at times it looked as though the prophet was going to be killed. Both Ezekiel and Daniel had their share of hardships, but the Lord delivered them. And even those who were not delivered, who died for the faith, received that special reward for those who are true to Him.

Why is it that those who "speak in the name of the Lord" often must endure difficult trials? It is so that their lives might back up their messages. The impact of a faithful, godly life carries much power. We need to remind ourselves that our patience in times of suffering is a testimony to others around us.

But have not many faithful Christians suffered and died without any notice or recognition? Yes, but when Jesus returns, these "obscure heroes" will receive their rewards. The prophets were killed and buried, but today their names are honored. When our Lord comes again, He will bring His reward with Him (Rev. 22:12).

This example that James used from the Old Testament prophets ought to encourage us to spend more time in the Bible, getting acquainted with these heroes of faith. "For everything that was written in the past was written to teach us, so that through endurance and the encouragement of the Scriptures we might have hope" (Rom. 15:4, NIV). The better we know the Bible, the more God can encourage us in the difficult experiences of life. The important thing is that, like the farmer, we keep working, and, like the prophets, we keep witnessing, no matter how trying the circumstances may be.

Job (5:11)

"As you know, we consider blessed those who have persevered" (5:11, NIV). But you cannot persevere unless there is a trial in your life. There can be no victories without battles; there can be no peaks without valleys. If you want the blessing, you must be prepared to carry the burden and fight the battle.

I once heard a young Christian pray, "O Lord, please teach me the deep truths of Thy Word! I want to be lifted up to the heavens to hear and see the wonderful things that are there!" It was a sincere prayer, but the young man did not realize what he was praying. Paul went to the third heaven and learned things too marvelous for words; and as a result, *God had to give Paul a thorn in the flesh to keep him humbl*e (2 Cor. 12:1-10). God has to balance privileges with responsibilities, blessings with burdens, or else you and I will become spoiled, pampered children.

When do "blessings" come? In the midst of trials we may experience God's blessings, as did

the three Hebrew children in the fiery furnace
(Dan. 3); but James taught that there is a blessing
after we have endured. His example was Job.

The Book of Job is a long book, and the chapters
are filled with speeches that, to the Western mind,
seem long and tedious. In the first three chapters
you have *Job's distress:* he loses his wealth, his
family (except for his wife, and she told him to
commit suicide), and his health. In chapters 4—31
we read *Job's defense,* as he debates with his
three friends and answers their false accusations.
Chapters 38—42 present *Job's deliverance:* first God
humbles Job, and then He honors Job and gives
him twice as much as he had before.

In studying the experience of Job, it is important
to remember that *Job did not know what was
going on "behind the scenes" between God and
Satan.* Job's friends accused him of being a sinner
and a hypocrite. "There must be some terrible sin
in your life," they argued, "or God would never
have permitted this suffering." Job disagreed with
them and maintained his innocence (but not perfection) during the entire conversation. The friends
were wrong: God had no cause against Job (Job
2:3), and in the end, God rebuked the friends for
telling lies about Job (Job 42:7).

It is difficult to find a greater example of suffering than Job. Circumstances were against him,
for he lost his wealth and his health. He also lost
his beloved children. His wife was against him,
for she said, "Curse God and die" (Job 2:9). His
friends were against him, for they accused him of
being a hypocrite, deserving of the judgment of
God. And it seemed like God was against him!
When Job cried out for answers to his questions,
there was no reply from heaven.

Yet, Job endured. Satan predicted that Job would get impatient with God and abandon his faith, but that did not happen. It is true that Job questioned God's will, but Job did not forsake his faith in the Lord. "Though He slay me, I will hope in Him. Nevertheless, I will argue my ways before Him" (Job 13:15, NASB). Job was so sure of God's perfections that he persisted in arguing with Him, even though he did not understand all that God was doing. That is endurance.

God made a covenant with Israel that He would bless them if they would obey His laws. (See Deut. 11.) This led to the idea that, if you were wealthy and comfortable, you were blessed of God; but if you were suffering and poor, you were cursed of God. Sad to say, many people have that same erroneous idea today. When Jesus said it was difficult for a rich man to enter heaven, the disciples were shocked. "Who then can be saved?" they asked (Matt. 19:23-26) "The rich are especially blessed of God," they were saying. "If *they* can't make it, nobody can!"

The Book of Job refutes that idea; for Job was a righteous man, *and yet he suffered*. God found no evil in him, and even Satan could not find any. Job's friends could not prove their accusations. Job teaches us that God has higher purposes in suffering than the punishing of sin. Job's experience paved the way for Jesus, the perfect Son of God who suffered, not for His own sins, but for the sins of the world.

In Job's case, what was "the end [purpose] of the Lord"? *To reveal Himself as full of pity and tender mercy.* Certainly, there were other results from Job's experience, for God never wastes the sufferings of His saints. Job met God in a new and deeper way (Job 42:1-6), and, after that, Job received greater blessings from the Lord.

"But if God is so merciful," someone may argue, "why didn't He protect Job from all that suffering to begin with?" To be sure, there are mysteries to God's working that our finite minds cannot fathom; but this we know: God was glorified and Job was purified through this difficult experience. If there is nothing to endure, you cannot learn endurance.

What did Job's story mean to the believers James wrote to, and what does it mean to us today? It means that some of the trials of life are caused directly by satanic opposition. God permits Satan to try His children, but He always limits the extent of the enemy's power (Job 1:12 and 2:6). When you find yourself in the fire, remember that God keeps His gracious hand on the thermostat! "But He knoweth the way that I take: when He hath tried me, I shall come forth as gold" (Job 23:10).

Satan wants us to get impatient with God, for an impatient Christian is a powerful weapon in the devil's hands. You will recall from our study of chapter 1 that Moses' impatience robbed him of a trip to the Holy Land; Abraham's impatience led to the birth of Ishmael, the enemy of the Jews; and Peter's impatience almost made him a murderer. When Satan attacks us, it is easy for us to get impatient and run ahead of God and lose God's blessing as a result.

What is the answer? "My grace is sufficient for thee!" (2 Cor. 12:7-9) Paul's thorn in the flesh was a "messenger of Satan." Paul could have fought it, given up under it, or tried to deny that the thorn existed; but he did not. Instead, he trusted God for the grace he needed; and he turned

Satan's weapon into a tool for the building up of his own spiritual life.

When you find yourself in the furnace, go to the throne of grace and receive from the Lord all the grace you need to endure (Heb. 4:14-16). Remind yourself that the Lord has a gracious purpose in all of this suffering, and that He will work out His purposes in His time and for His glory. You are not a robot caught in the jaws of fate. You are a loving child of God, privileged to be a part of a wonderful plan. There is a difference!

The exhortation in verse 12 seems out of place; for what does "speaking oaths" have to do with the problem of suffering? If you have ever suffered, you know the answer: it is easy to say things you do not mean, and even make bargains with God, when you are going through difficulties. Go back to Job for an example. The patriarch said, "Naked came I out of my mother's womb, and naked shall I return thither: the Lord gave, and the Lord hath taken away; blessed be the name of the Lord. In all this Job sinned not, nor charged God foolishly" (Job 1:21-22). Job did curse the day he was born (Job 3:1ff), but he never cursed God or spoke with a foolish oath. Neither did he try to bargain with God.

Surely James is reminding us of our Lord's teaching in the Sermon on the Mount (Matt. 5:34-37). The Jews were great ones for using various oaths to back up their statements. They were careful, however, not to use the name of God in their oaths, lest they blaspheme God. So, they would swear by heaven, or earth, or Jerusalem, or even by their own heads! But Jesus taught that it is impossible to avoid God in such oaths. Heaven is His throne, earth is His footstool, and Jerusalem is

the "city of the great King." As for swearing by
your head, what good is it? "Thou canst not make
one hair black or white" (Matt. 5:36)—or even
keep one hair on your head.

It is a basic principle that true Christian character requires few words. The person who must
use many words (including oaths) to convince us
has something wrong with his character and must
bolster this weakness by using words. If you are a
true Christian, with integrity, then all you have to
say is "Yes" or "No" and people will believe you.
Jesus warns us that anything more than this is from
the evil one.

One of the purposes of suffering is the building
of character. Certainly Job was a better man for
having gone through the furnace. (James explained
this process to us, 1:2-12.) If words are a test of
character, then oaths would indicate that there is
yet work to be done. When Peter poured out those
oaths in the courtyard (Matt. 26:71), he was giving
evidence that his character was still in need of a
transformation.

As you review this section, you can see the
practicality of it. James wanted to encourage us
to be patient in times of suffering. Like the farmer,
we are waiting for a spiritual harvest, for fruit
that will glorify God. Like the prophets, we look
for opportunities for witness, to share the truth of
God. And, like Job, we wait for the Lord to fulfill
His loving purpose, knowing that He will never
cause His children to suffer needlessly. And, like
Job, we shall have a clearer vision of the Lord and
come to know Him better for having been in the
furnace of affliction.

"Be patient, for the coming of the Lord draweth
nigh!"

13

Let Us Pray

(JAMES 5:13–20)

The gift of speech is a marvelous blessing, if it is used to the glory of God. As we have seen, James had a great deal to say about the tongue; and this chapter is no exception. He mentioned some of the lowest uses of the tongue: complaining (5:9) and swearing (5:12). But he also named some of the highest uses of the tongue: proclaiming God's Word (5:10) and praying and praising God (5:13).

Prayer is certainly a high and holy privilege. To think that, as God's children, we can come freely and boldly to His throne and share with Him our needs! Seven times in this section James mentioned prayer. The mature Christian is prayerful in the troubles of life. Instead of complaining about his situation, he talks to God about it; and God hears and answers his prayers. "Taking it to the Lord in prayer" is certainly a mark of spiritual maturity.

In this section, James encourages us to pray by

describing four situations in which God answers prayer.

Prayer for the Suffering (5:13)

The word *afflicted* means "suffering in difficult circumstances." The phrase "in trouble" is a good translation. Paul used this word to describe the circumstances he was in as he suffered for the Gospel's sake (2 Tim. 2:9). As God's people go through life, they often must endure difficulties that are not the results of sin or the chastening of God.

What should we do when we find ourselves in such trying circumstances? We must not grumble and criticize the saints who are having an easier time of it (James 5:9); nor should we blame the Lord. We should pray, asking God for the wisdom we need to understand the situation and use it to His glory (James 1:5).

Prayer can remove affliction, if that is God's will. But prayer can also give us the grace we need to endure troubles and use them to accomplish God's perfect will. *God can transform troubles into triumphs.* "He giveth more grace" (James 4:6). Paul prayed that God might change his circumstances, but instead, God gave Paul the grace he needed to turn his weakness into strength (2 Cor. 12:7-10). Our Lord prayed in Gethsemane that the cup might be removed, and it was not; yet the Father gave Him the strength He needed to go to the cross and die for our sins.

James indicated that everybody does not go through troubles at the same time: "Is any merry? Let him sing psalms" (5:13). God balances our lives and gives us hours of suffering and days of singing. The mature Christian knows how to sing *while he is suffering.* (Anybody can sing after the trouble has passed.) God is able to give "songs in the night" (Job 35:10). He did this for Paul and Silas when they were suffering in that Philippian jail. "And at midnight Paul and Silas prayed, and sang praises unto God" (Acts 16:25).

Praying and singing were important elements in worship in the early church, and they should be important to us. Our singing ought to be an expression of our inner spiritual life. The believer's praise should be intelligent (1 Cor. 14:15) and not just the mouthing of words or ideas that mean nothing to him. It should come from the heart (Eph. 5:19) and be motivated by the Holy Spirit (Eph. 5:18). Christian singing must be based on the Word of God (Col. 3:16) and not simply on the clever ideas of men. If a song is not biblical, it is not acceptable to God.

Prayer for the Sick (5:14-16)

I do not think that James gave us a blanket formula for healing the sick. In the churches I have pastored, the elders and I have prayed for the sick, and sometimes God has given healing. But other times, He has not seen fit to heal the person. I recall two cases within one week of each other: the one lady was restored in an almost miraculous way, but the other one had to enter the hospital for surgery, and eventually the Lord called her home.

What are the special characteristics of this case that James is describing?

The person is sick because of sin (15b-16). The Greek text says, "if he has been constantly sinning." This parallels 1 Corinthians 11:30, "For this cause many are weak and sickly among you, and many sleep" (have died). James has described a church member who is sick because he is being disciplined by God. This explains why the elders of the assembly are called: the man cannot go to church to confess his sins, so he asks the spiritual leaders to come to him. The leaders would be in charge of the discipline of the congregation.

The person confesses his sins (5:16). In the early church, the believers practiced church discipline. First Corinthians 5 is a good example. Paul told the believers at Corinth to dismiss the sinning member from the assembly until he repented of his sins and made things right. The little word "therefore" belongs in James 5:16—"Confess your sins therefore to one another, and pray for one another, that you may be healed" (literal translation). The word *faults* in the Authorized Version gives the impression that the man's deeds were not too evil; they were only faults. But it is the word *hamartia* that James used, and this word means "sin." It is the same word used in James 1:15, where the subject is definitely sin.

The person is healed by "the prayer of faith" *(5:15).* It is not the anointing that heals, but the praying. The Greek word translated "anointing" is a medicinal term; it could be translated "massaging." This may be an indication that James suggests using available means for healing along with asking the Lord for His divine touch. God can heal with or without means; in each case, it is God who does the healing.

But what is "the prayer of faith" that heals the sick? The answer is in 1 John 5:14-15—"And this is the confidence that we have in Him, that, if we ask anything according to His will, He heareth us: and if we know that He hear us, whatsoever we ask, we know that we have the petitions that we desired of Him." The "prayer of faith" is a prayer offered *when you know the will of God.* The elders would seek the mind of God in the matter, and then pray according to His will.

As I visit the sick among my congregation, I do not always know how to pray for them. (Paul had the same problem; read Rom. 8:26.) Is it God's will to heal? Is God planning to call His child home? I do not know; therefore, I must pray, "If it is Your will, heal your child." Those who claim that God heals every case, and that it is not His will for His children to be sick, are denying both Scripture and experience. But where we have the inner conviction from the Word and the Spirit that it is God's will to heal, then we can pray "the prayer of faith" and expect God to work.

Keep in mind that it is not one individual who is praying: it is the body of elders—spiritual men of God—who seek God's will and pray. James does not instruct the believer to send for a faith healer. The matter is in the hands of the leaders of the local church.

There are some practical lessons from this section that we must not overlook. For one thing, disobedience to God can lead to sickness. This was David's experience when he tried to hide his sins (Ps. 32). Second, sin affects the whole church. We can never sin alone, for sin has a way of growing and infecting others. This man had to confess his sins to the church because he had sinned against the church. Third, there is healing (physical and spiritual) when sin is dealt with. "He that covereth his sins shall not prosper, but whoso confesseth and forsaketh them shall find mercy" (Prov. 28:13). James wrote, "Make it a habit to confess your sins to each other" (literal translation). Do not hide sin or delay confession.

The "confessing" that James wrote about is done among the saints. He was not suggesting confessing our sins to a preacher or priest. We confess our sins first of all to the Lord (1 John 1:9), but we must also confess them to those who have been affected by them. *We must never confess sin beyond the circle of that sin's influence.* Private sin requires private confession; public sin requires public confession. It is wrong for Christians to "hang dirty wash in public," for such "confessing" might do more harm than the original sin.

Prayer for the Nation (5:17-18)

James cited Elijah as an example of a "righteous man" whose prayers released power. "The prayer of a righteous man is powerful and effective" (5:16, NIV).

The background of this incident is found in 1 Kings 17—18. Wicked King Ahab and Jezebel, his queen, had led Israel away from the Lord and into the worship of Baal. God punished the nation by holding back the rain that they needed (see Deut. 28:12, 23). For three and one-half years, the heavens were as brass and the earth unable to produce the crops so necessary for life.

Then Elijah challenged the priests of Baal on Mt. Carmel. All day long the priests cried out to their god, but no answer came. At the time of the evening sacrifice, Elijah repaired the altar and prepared the sacrifice. He prayed but once, and fire came from heaven to consume the sacrifice. He had proved that Jehovah was the true God.

But the nation still needed rain. Elijah went to the top of Carmel and fell down before the Lord in prayer. He prayed and sent his servant seven times to see if there was evidence of rain; and the seventh time his servant saw a little cloud. Before long, there was a great rain, and the nation was saved.

Do we need "showers of blessing" today? We certainly do!

"But Elijah was a special prophet of God," we might argue. "We can expect God to answer his prayers in a wonderful way."

"Elijah was a man just like us," stated James (5:17, NIV). He was not perfect; in fact, right after his victory on Mount Carmel, Elijah became afraid and discouraged and ran away. But he was a "righteous man," that is, obedient to the Lord and trusting Him. God's promises of answered prayer are for all his children, not just for ones we may call the spiritual elite.

Elijah prayed in faith, for God told him He would send the rain (1 Kings 18:1). "Prayer," said Robert Law, "is not getting man's will done in heaven. It's getting God's will done on earth." You cannot separate the Word of God and prayer, for in His Word He gives us the promises that we claim when we pray.

Elijah was not only believing in his praying, but he was persistent. "He prayed . . . and he prayed again" (James 5:17-18). On Mount Carmel, Elijah continued to pray for rain until his servant reported "a cloud the size of a man's hand." Too many times we fail to get what God promises because we stop praying. It is true that we are not heard "for our much praying" (Matt. 6:7); but there is a difference between vain repetitions and true believing persistence in prayer. Our Lord prayed three times in the Garden, and Paul prayed three

times that his thorn in the flesh might be taken
from him.

Elijah was determined and concerned in his
praying. "He prayed earnestly" (James 5:17, NIV)
The literal Greek reads "and he prayed in prayer."
Many people do not pray in their prayers. They
just lazily say religious words, and their hearts
are not in their prayers.

A church member was "praying around the
world" in a prayer meeting, and one of the men
present was growing tired of the speech. Finally
the man cried out, "Ask Him something!" That is
what prayer is all about: "Ask Him something!"

Prayer power is the greatest power in the world
today. "Tremendous power is made available
through a good man's earnest prayer" (5:16, PH).
History shows how mankind has progressed from
manpower to horsepower, and then to dynamite
and TNT, and now to atomic power.

But greater than atomic power is prayer power.
Elijah prayed for his nation, and God answered
prayer. We need to pray for our nation today, that
God will bring conviction and revival, and that
"showers of blessing" will come to the land. One
of the first responsibilities of the local church is
to pray for government leaders (1 Tim. 2:1-3).

Prayer for the Straying (5:19-20)

While James did not specifically name prayer in
these verses, the implication is there. If we pray
for the afflicted and the sick, surely we must pray
for the brother who wanders from the truth.

These verses deal with our ministry to a fellow
believer who strays from the truth and gets into
sin. The verb *err* means "to wander," and suggests
a gradual moving away from the will of God. The

Old Testament term for this is "backsliding." Sad to say, we see this tragedy occurring in our churches regularly. Sometimes a brother is "overtaken in a fault" (Gal. 6:1); but usually the sin is the result of slow, gradual spiritual decline.

Such a condition is, of course, very dangerous. It is dangerous to the offender because he may be disciplined by the Lord (Heb. 12). He also faces the danger of committing "sin unto death" (1 John 5:16-17). God disciplined the sinning members of the Corinthian church, even to the point of taking some of them to heaven (1 Cor. 11:30).

But this backsliding is also dangerous to the church. A wandering offender can influence others and lead them astray. "One sinner destroys much good" (Ecc. 9:18, NASB). This is why the spiritual members of the church must step in and help the man who has wandered away.

The *origin of this problem* is found in the statement "wander from the truth" (James 5:19). The *truth* means, of course, the Word of God. "Thy Word is truth" (John 17:17). Unless the believer stays close to the truth, he will start to drift away. "For this reason we must pay much closer attention to what we have heard, lest we drift away from it" (Heb. 2:1, NASB). Jesus warned Peter that Satan was at hand to tempt him, and Peter refused to believe the Word. He even argued with the Lord! When he should have been praying, Peter was sleeping. No wonder he denied three times.

The *outcome* of this wandering is "sin" and possible "death" (James 5:20). The sinner here is a believer, not an unbeliever; and sin in the life of a Christian is worse than sin in the life of an believer. We expect unsaved people to si God expects His children to obey His W

What are we to do when we see a fellow believer wandering from the truth? We should pray for him, to be sure; but we must also seek to help him. He needs to be "converted"—turned back into the right path again. Do believers need to be converted? Yes, they do! Jesus said to Peter, "When thou art converted, strengthen thy brethren" (Luke 22:32).

It is important that we seek to win the lost, but it is also important to win the saved. If a brother has sinned against us, we should talk to him privately and seek to settle the matter. If he listens, then we have gained our brother (Matt. 18:15). That word *gained* means "won." It is the same word translated "get gain" in James 4:13. It is important to win the saved as well as the lost.

If we are going to help an erring brother, we must have an attitude of love, for "love shall cover the multitude of sins" (1 Peter 4:8). Both James and Peter learned this principle from Proverbs 10:12—"Hate stirreth up strife: but love covereth all sins."

This does not mean that love "sweeps the dirt under the carpet." Where there is love, there must also be truth ("speaking the truth in love" says Paul in Eph. 4:15); and where there is truth, there is honest confession of sin and cleansing from God. Love not only helps the offender to face his sins and deal with them, but love also assures the offender that those sins, once forgiven, are remembered no more.

While the basic interpretation of these verses is as I have explained, the application can be made to the lost sinner. After all, if a straying brother needs to be restored, how much more does a lost sinner need to be brought to the Saviour. If the wandering believer loses his life, he at least goes to heaven; but the lost sinner is condemned to an eternal hell.

"Seeking the lost" is a common Bible picture of soul-winning. In Luke 15, Jesus pictures the lost sheep, the lost coin, and the lost son, all of whom needed to be found and brought back to where they belonged. Our Lord also compared winning souls to catching fish (Mark 1:17). Peter caught one fish individually with his hook (Matt. 17:24-27), but he also worked with his helpers and used the nets to catch many fish at one time. There is a place for both personal and collective evangelism.

Proverbs 11:30 compares evangelism to hunting: "he that catcheth souls is wise" (literal translation). Sin is out to catch and kill (James 1:13-15), but we ought to be out to catch and make alive.

The soul-winner is also an ambassador of peace (2 Cor. 5:20). God has not declared war on this world; He has declared peace! One day He will declare war, and judgment will fall.

Both Zechariah 3:2 and Jude 23 picture the soul-winner as a fireman, pulling brands out of the burning. John Wesley applied Zechariah 3:2 to himself, for when he was but a child, he was pulled from a burning house when it looked as though it was too late. Sometimes we must take risks of love to snatch people from the fires of judgment.

Jesus compared evangelism to sowing and reaping (John 4:34-38) and Paul used the same illustration (1 Cor. 3:6-9). There are seasons of sowing and seasons of reaping; and many people are needed for the work. We are "laborers together with God" (1 Cor. 3:9). Both the sower and the reaper will receive their rewards, for there is competition in the Lord's fields.

This brings us to the end of our study

His emphasis has been spiritual maturity. This would be a good time for us to examine our own hearts to see how mature we really are. Here are a few questions to assist you:

1. Am I becoming more and more patient in the testings of life?

2. Do I play with temptation or resist it from the start?

3. Do I find joy in obeying the Word of God, or do I merely study it and learn it?

4. Are there any prejudices that shackle me?

5. Am I able to control my tongue?

6. Am I a peacemaker rather than a trouble-maker? Do people come to me for spiritual wisdom?

7. Am I a friend of God or a friend of the world?

8. Do I make plans without considering the will of God?

9. Am I selfish when it comes to money? Am I unfaithful in the paying of my bills?

10. Do I naturally depend on prayer when I find myself in some kind of trouble?

11. Am I the kind of person others seek for prayer support?

12. What is my attitude toward the wandering brother? Do I criticize and gossip, or do I seek to restore him in love?

Don't just grow old—grow up!